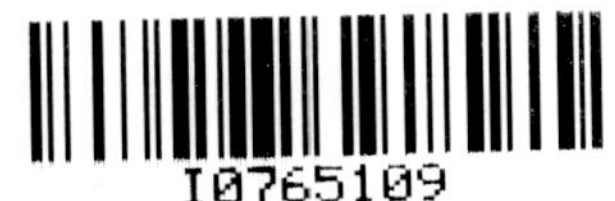

COLORING BOOK
FOR ADULTS
MANDALA

John Maramao

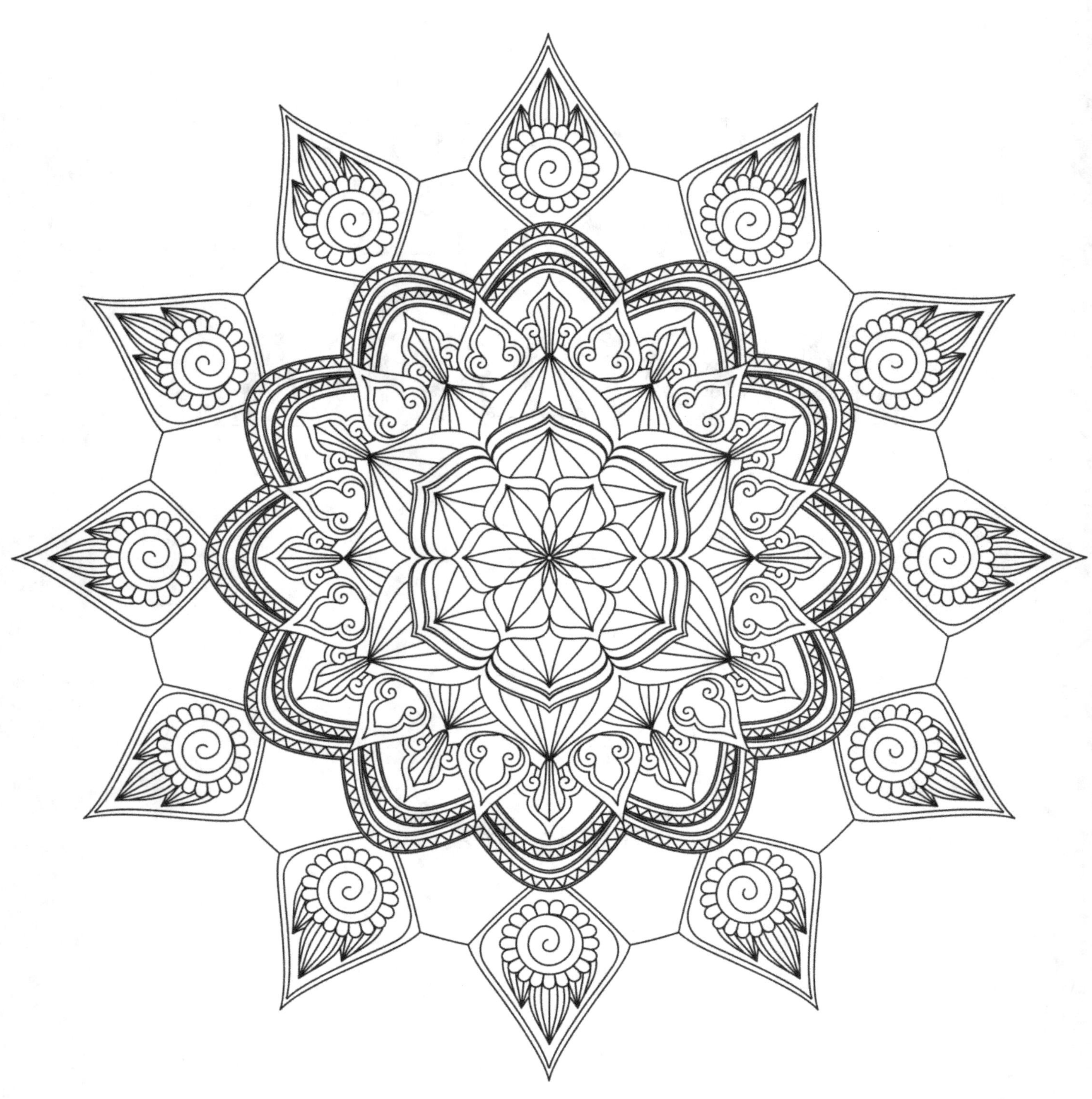

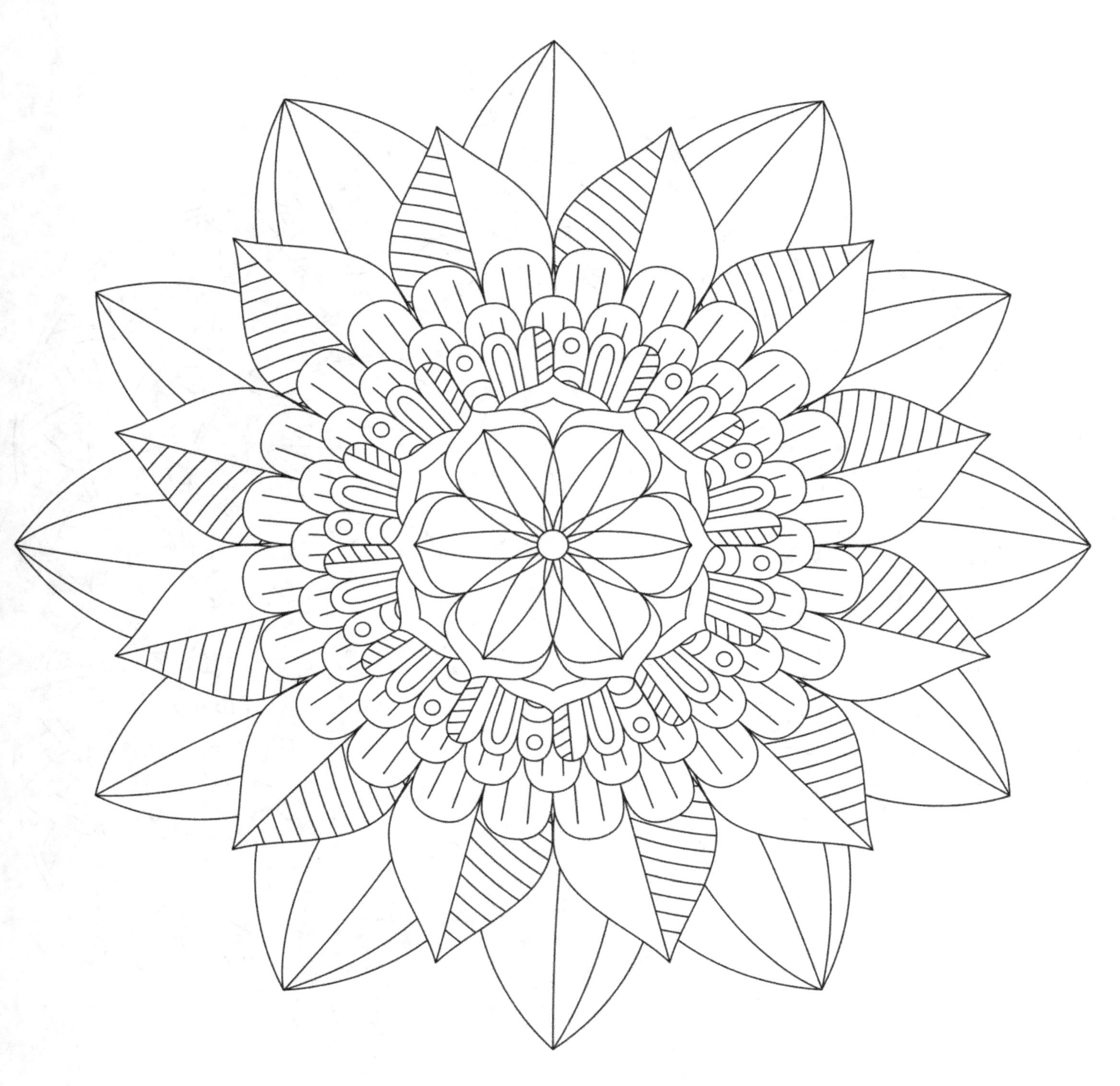

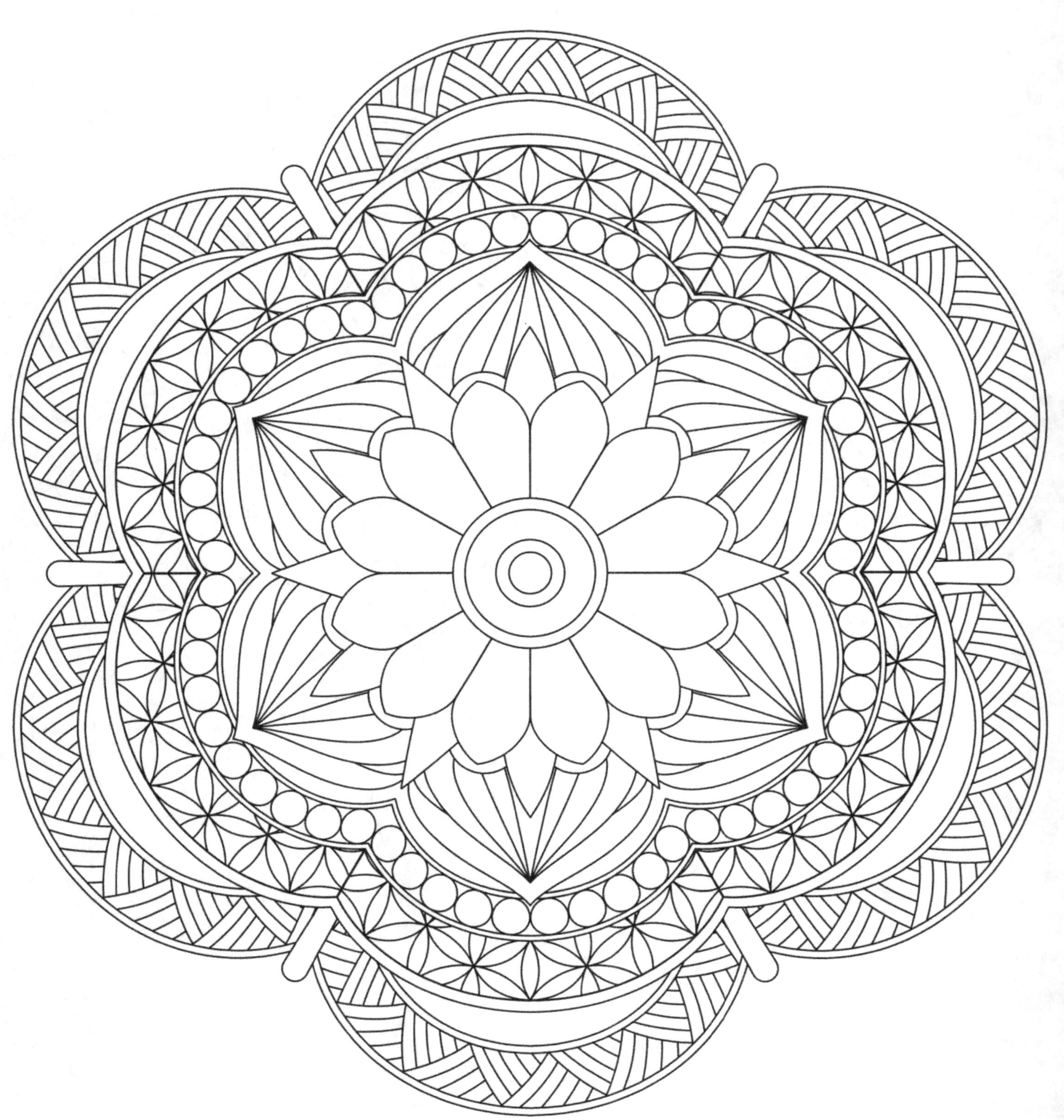

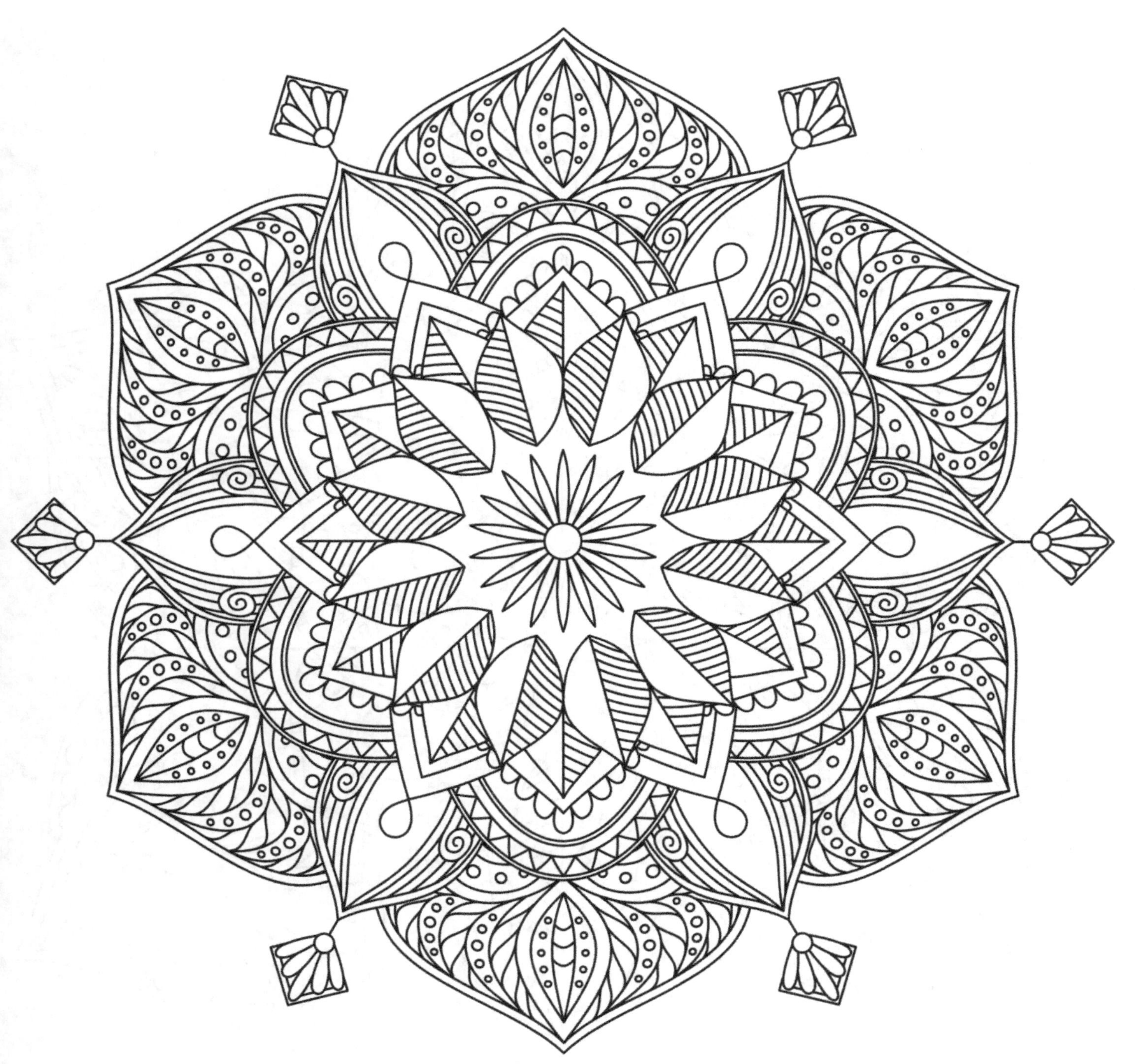

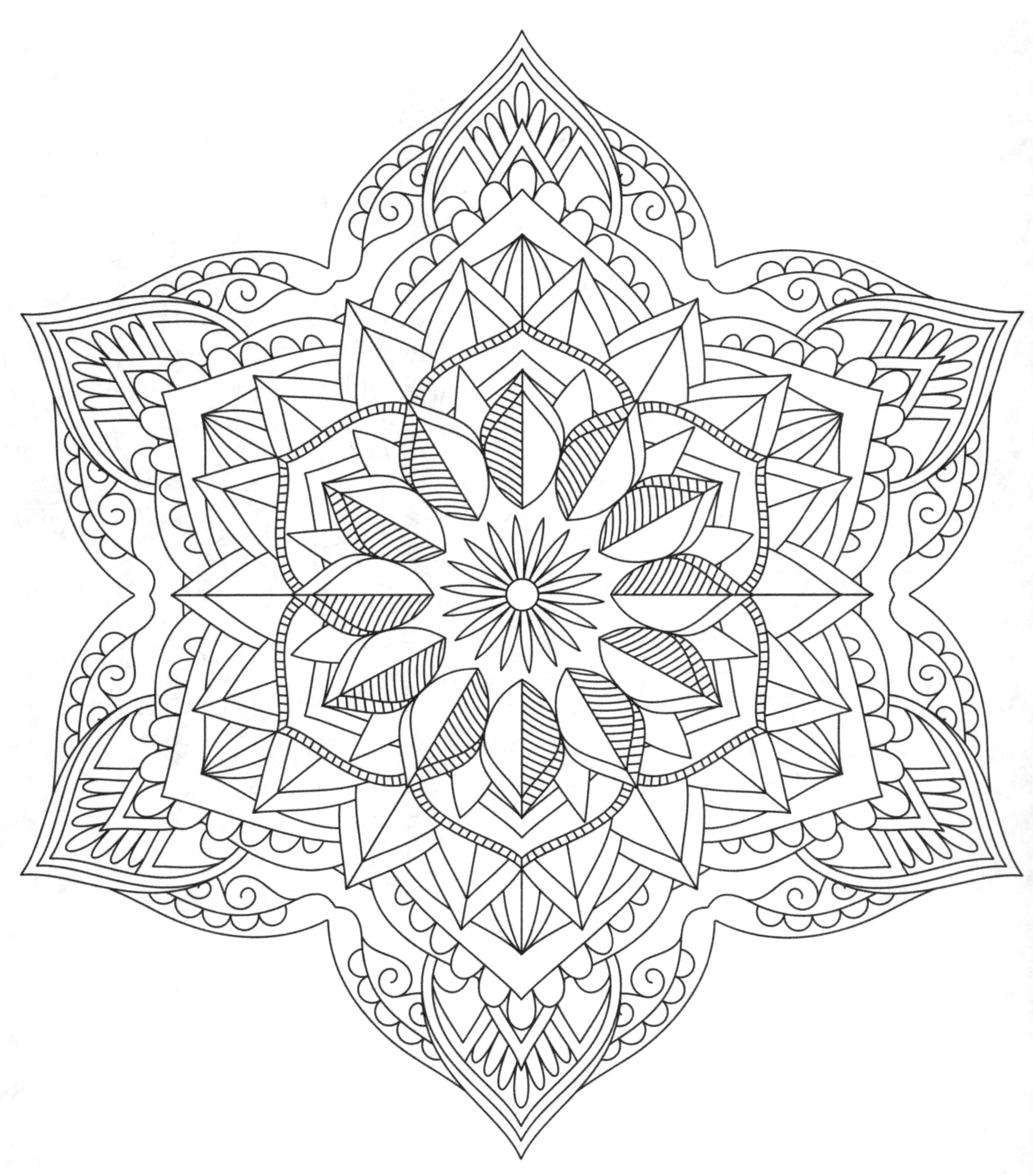

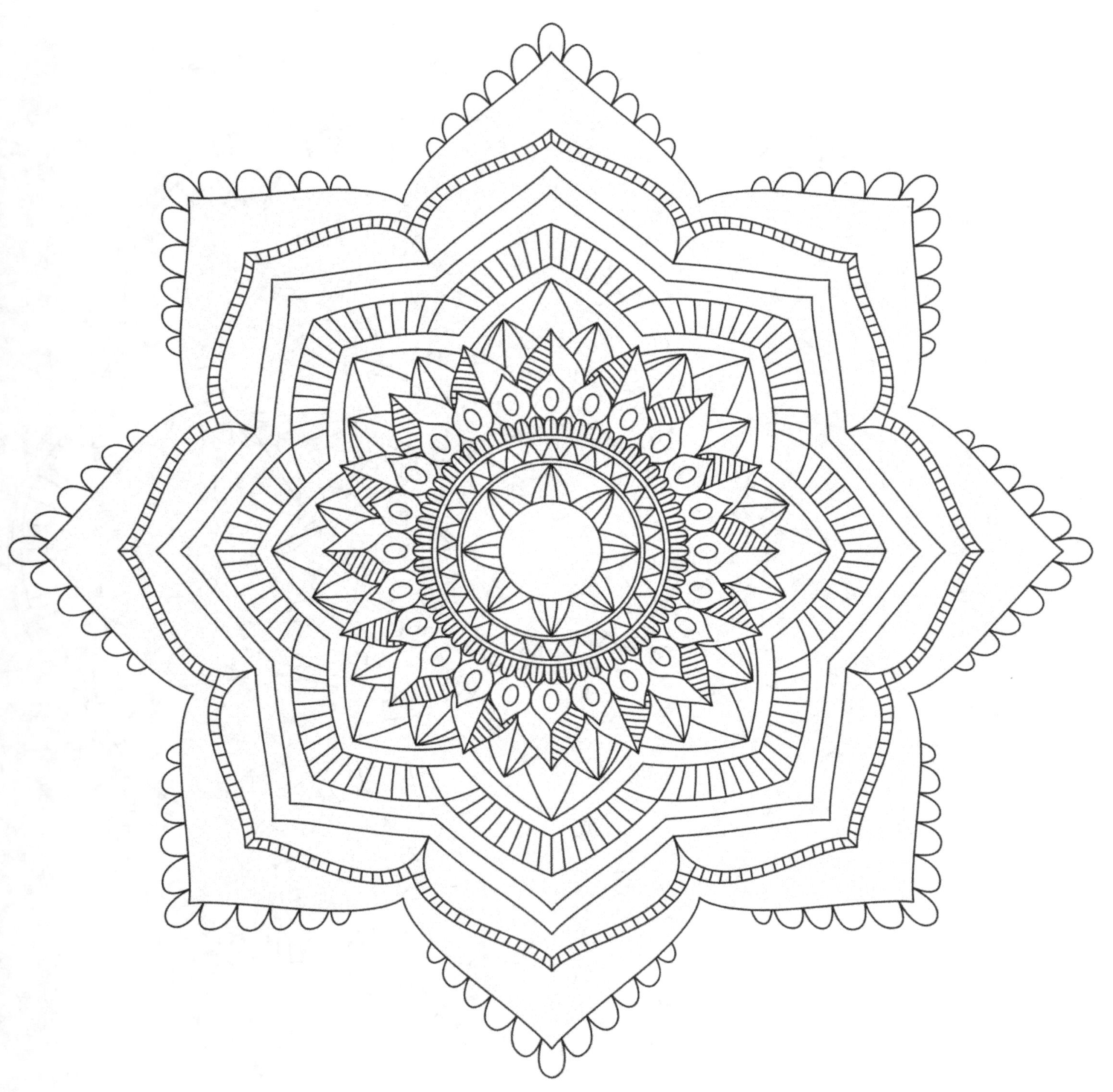

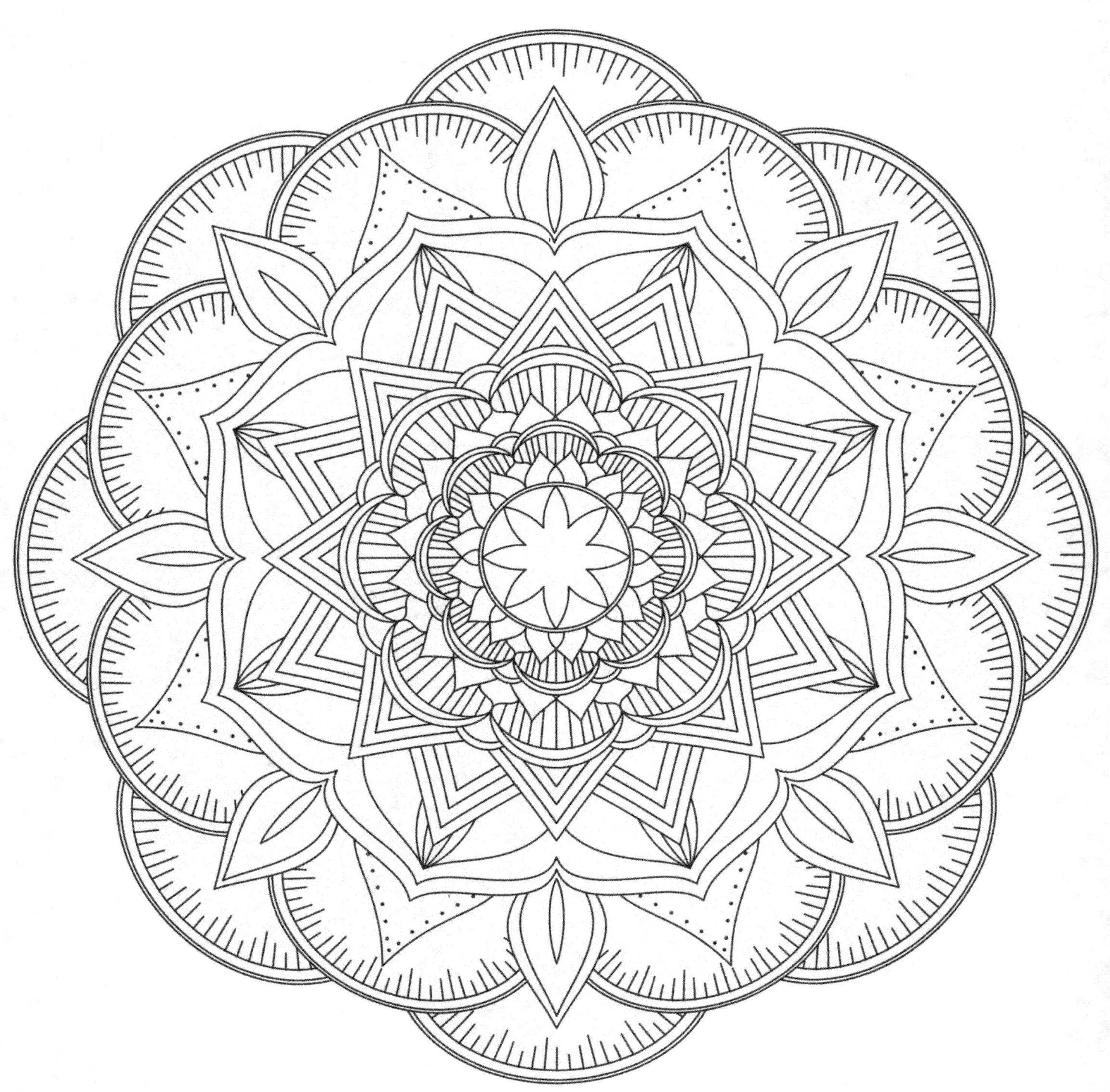

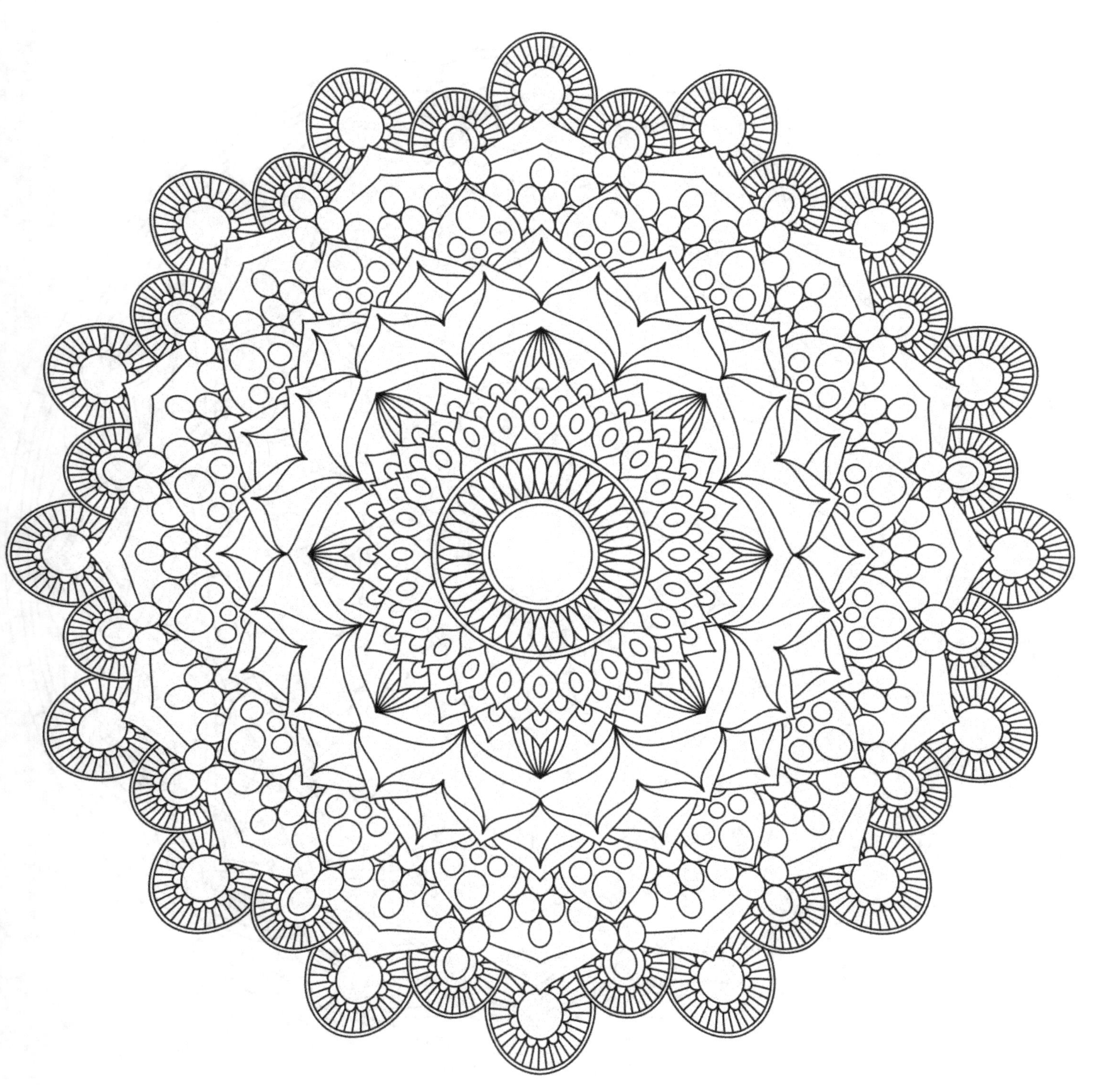

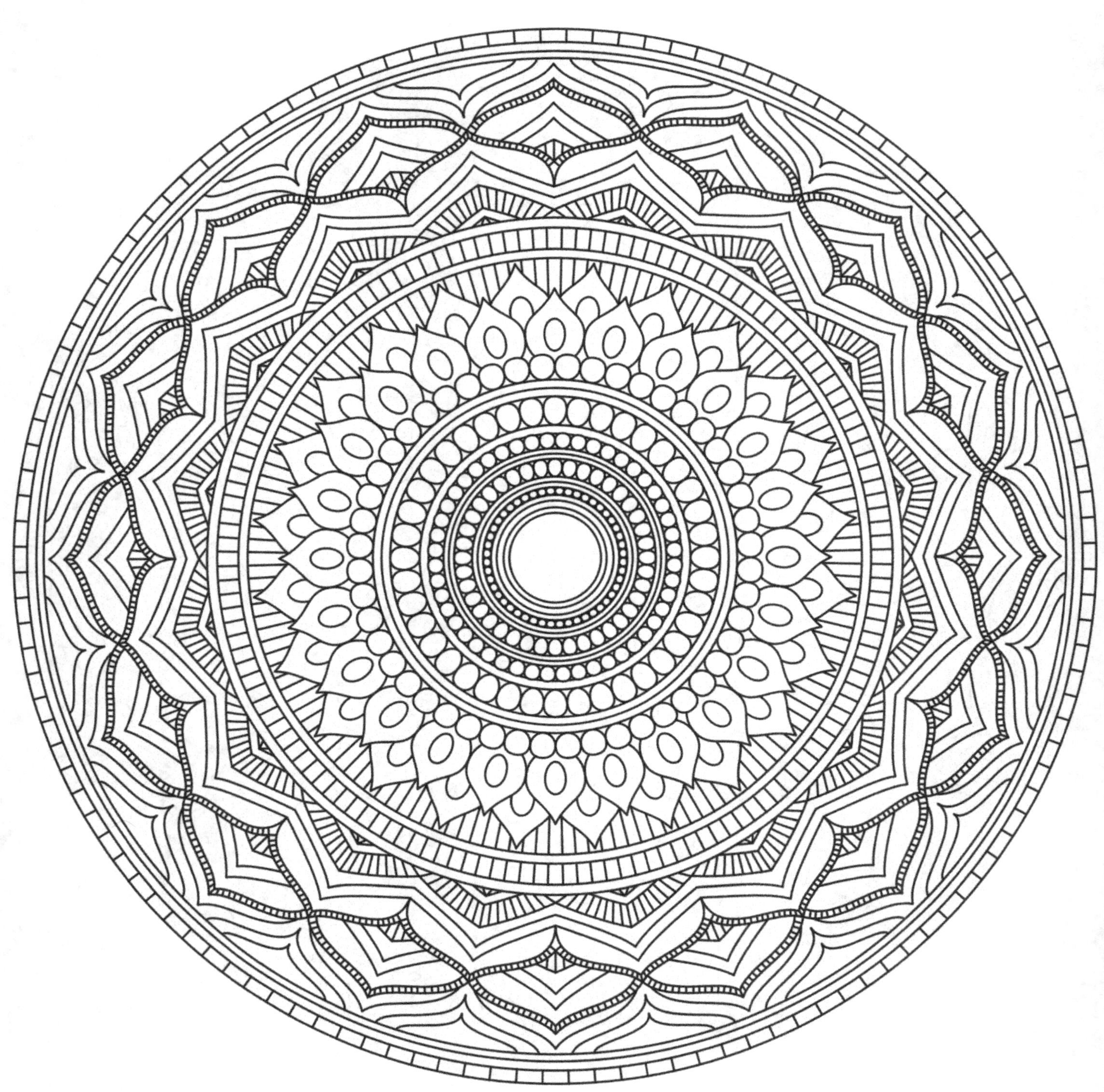

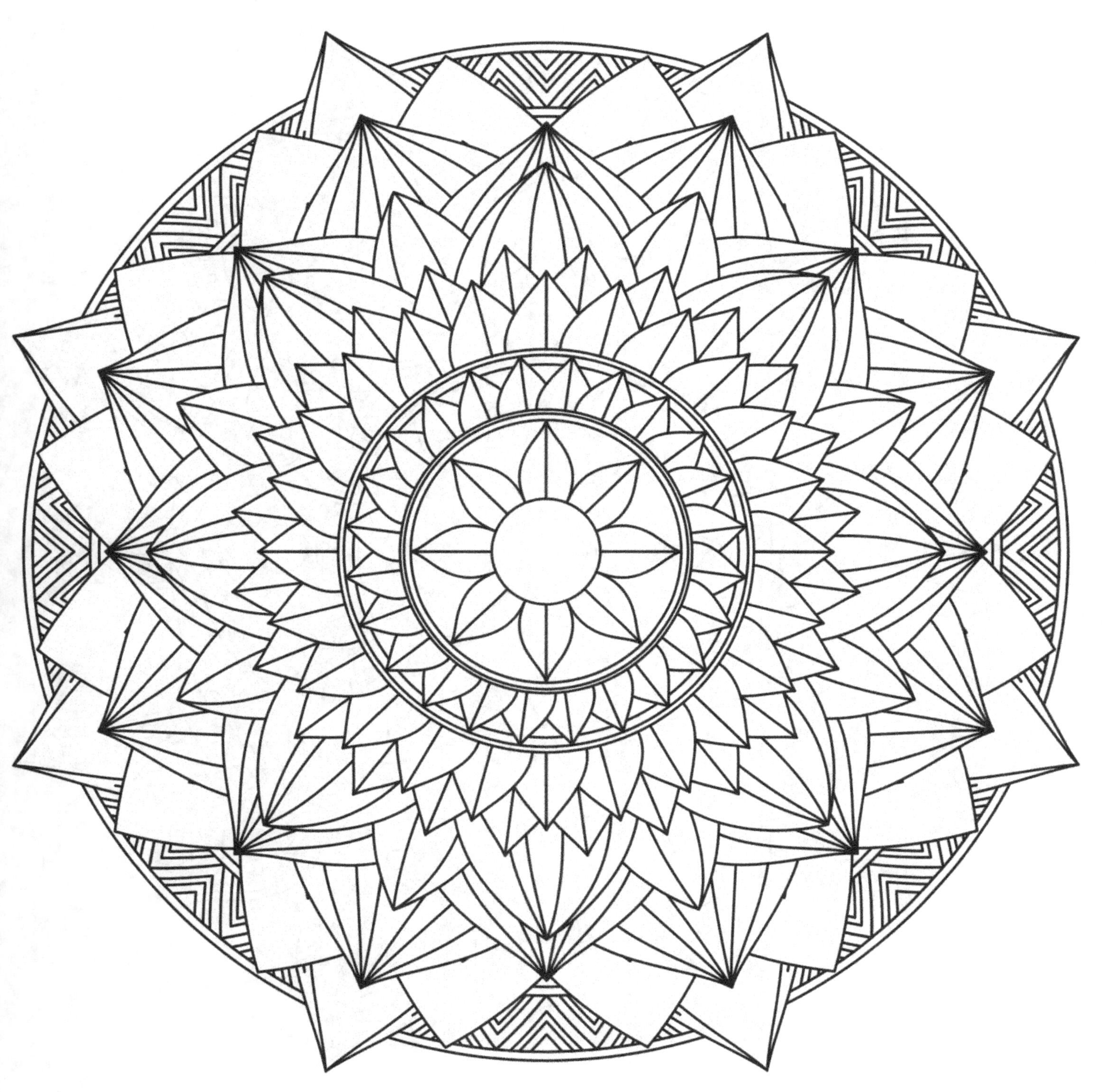

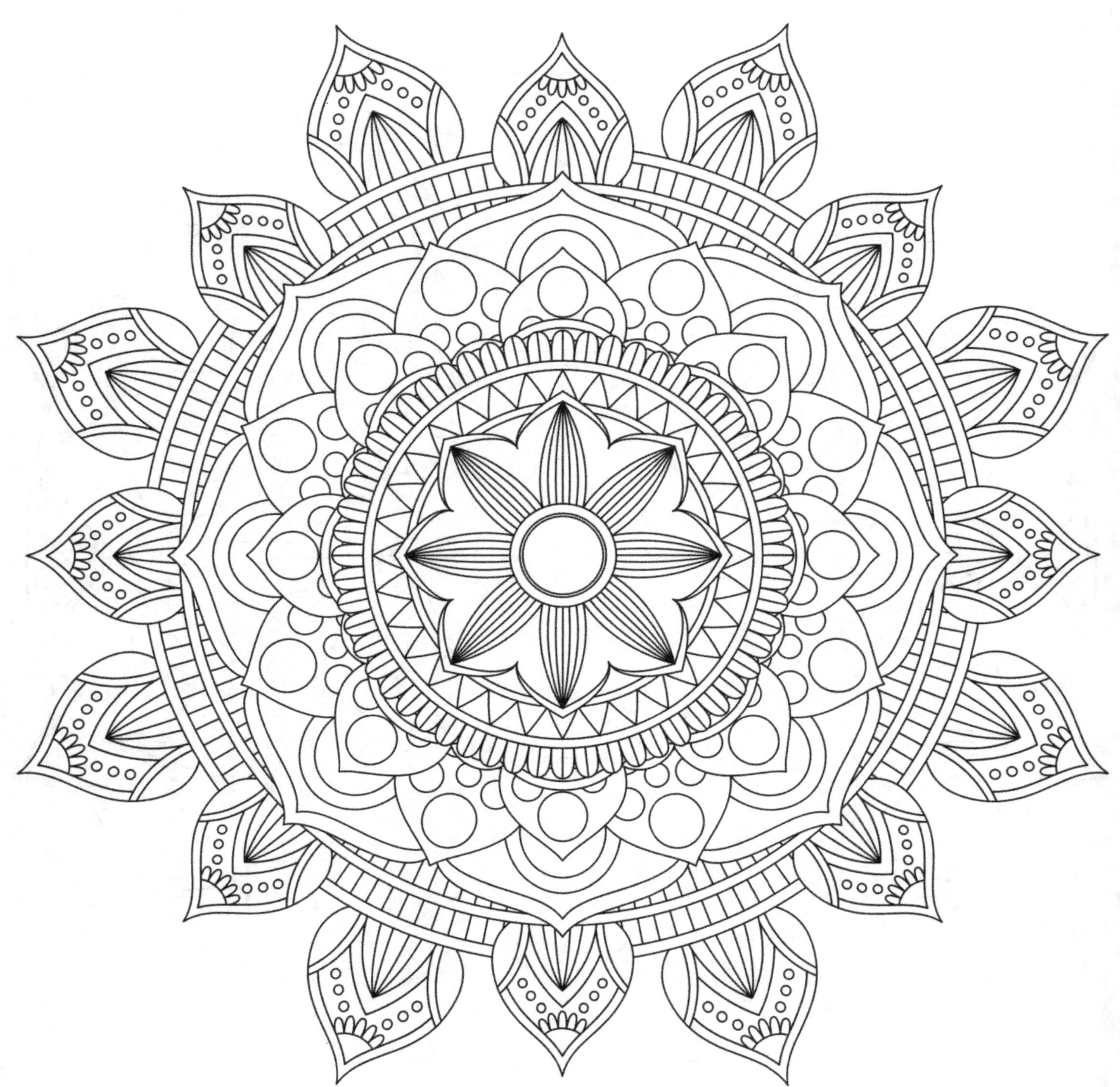

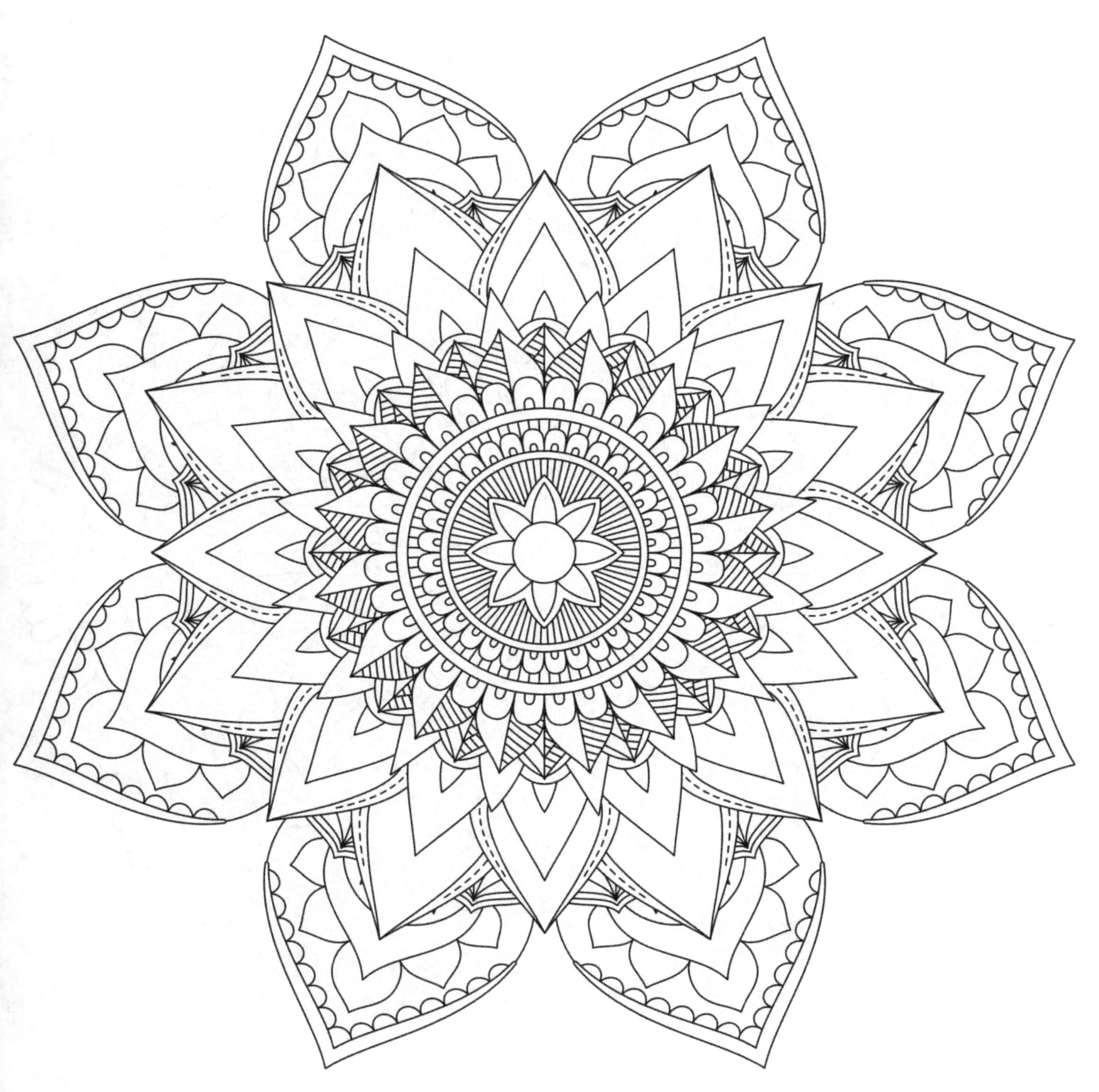

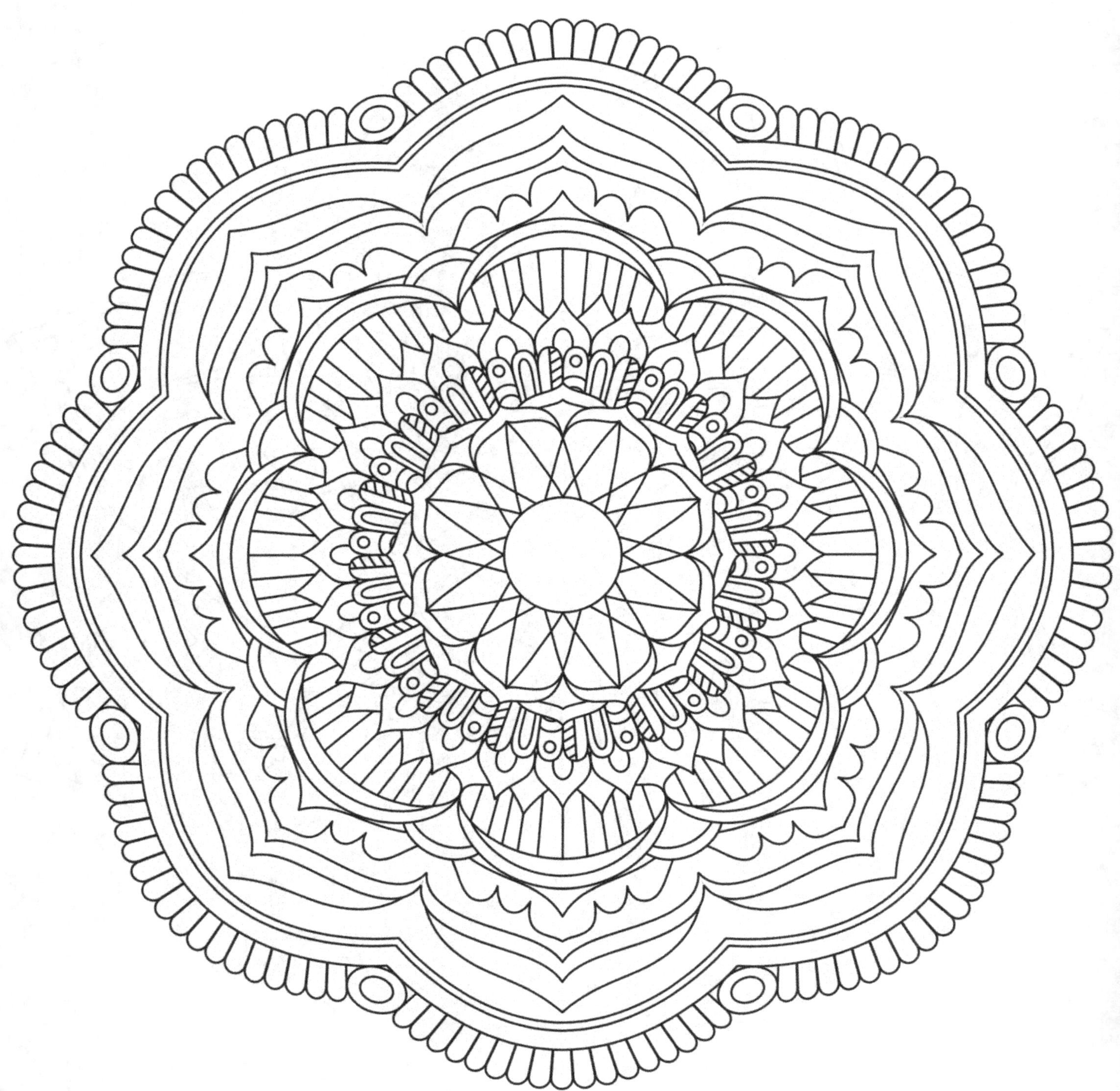

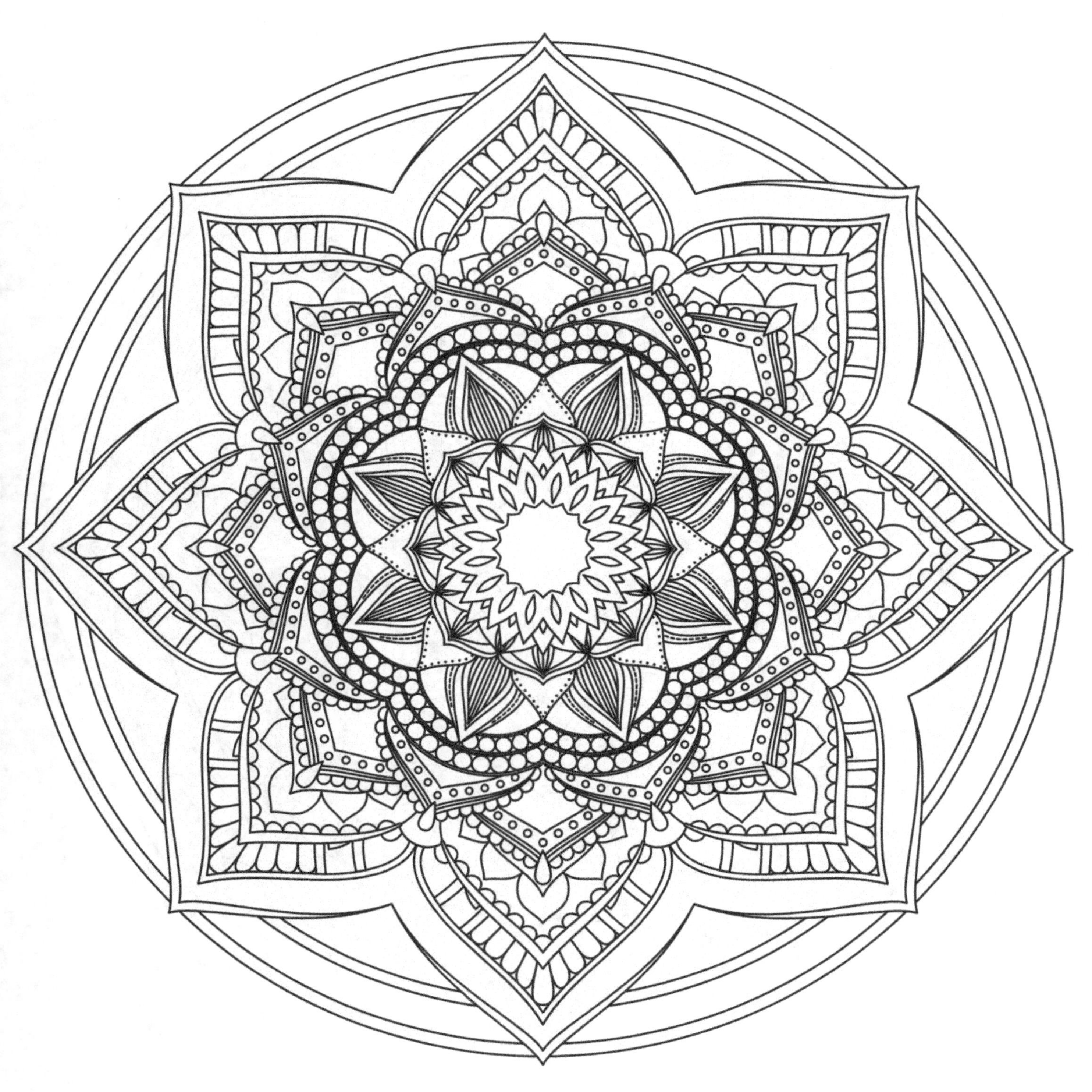

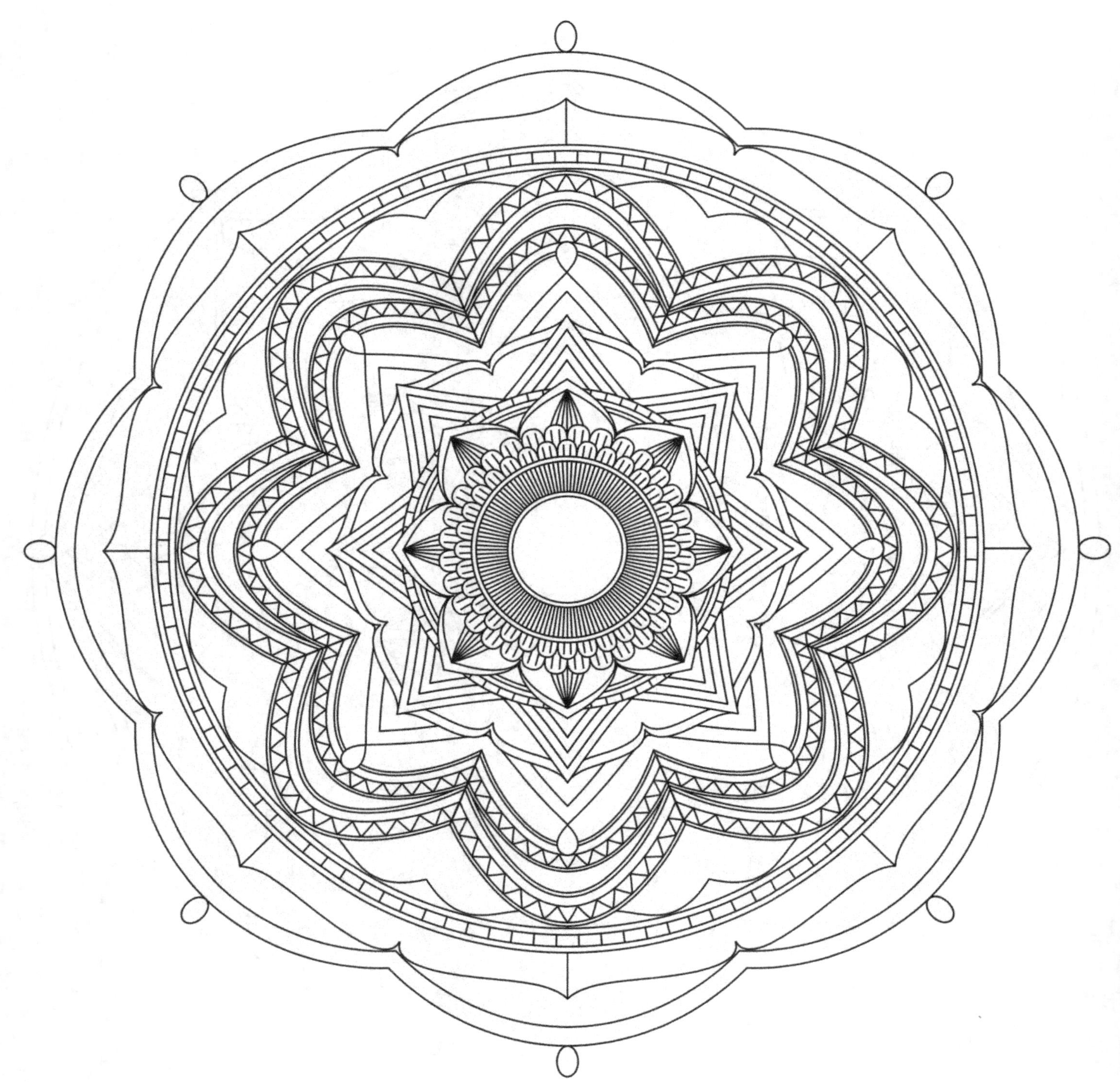

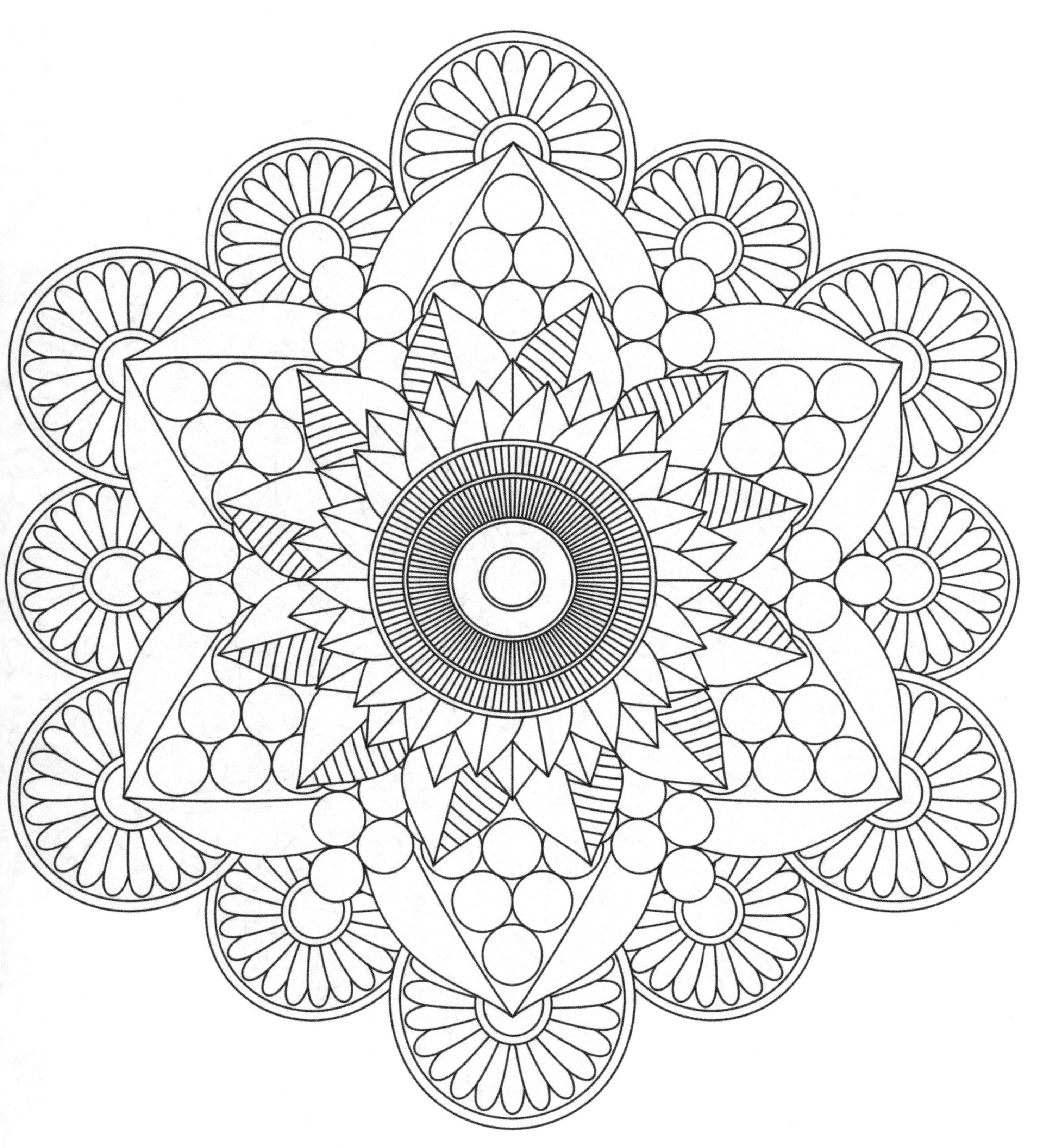

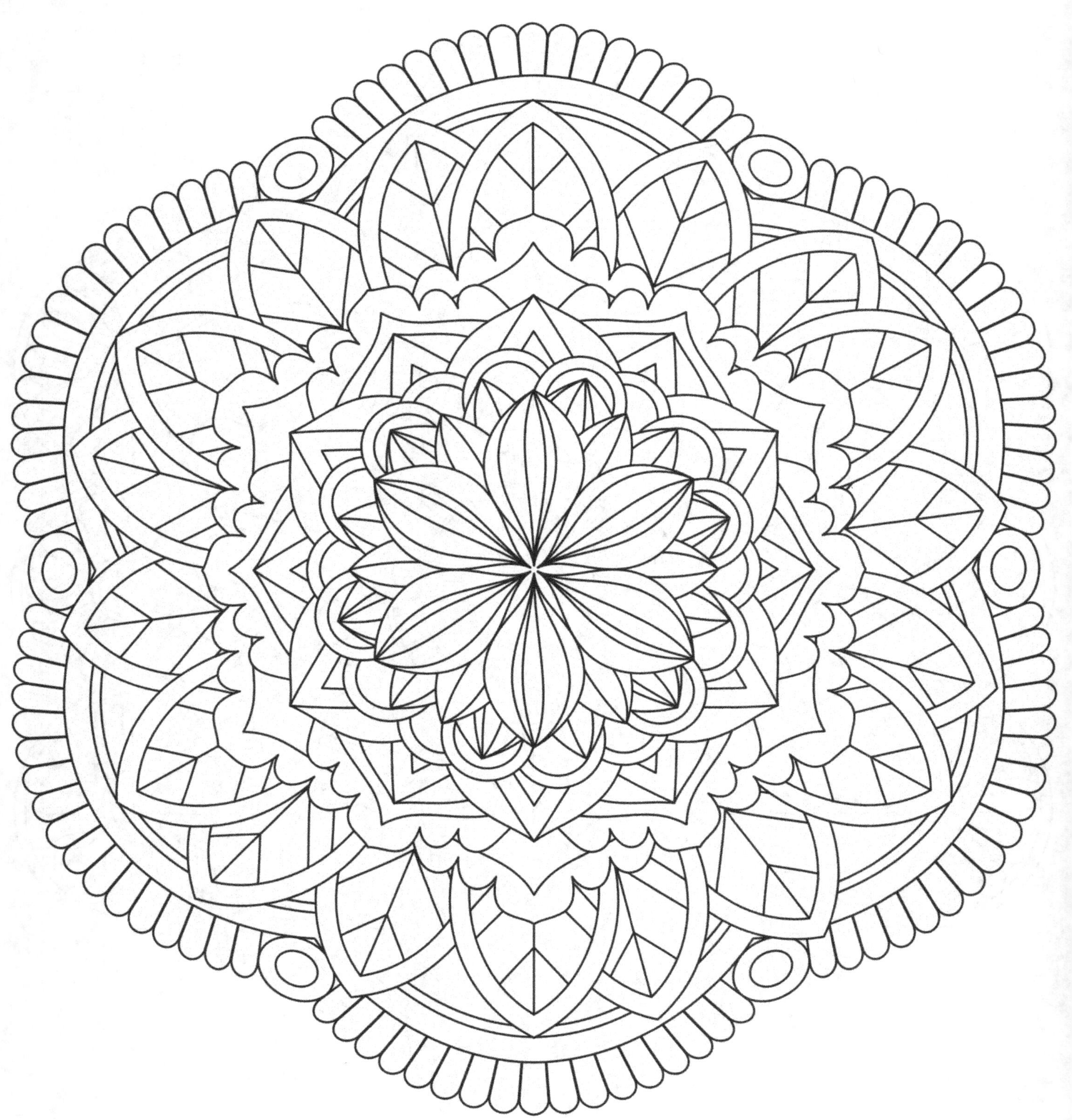

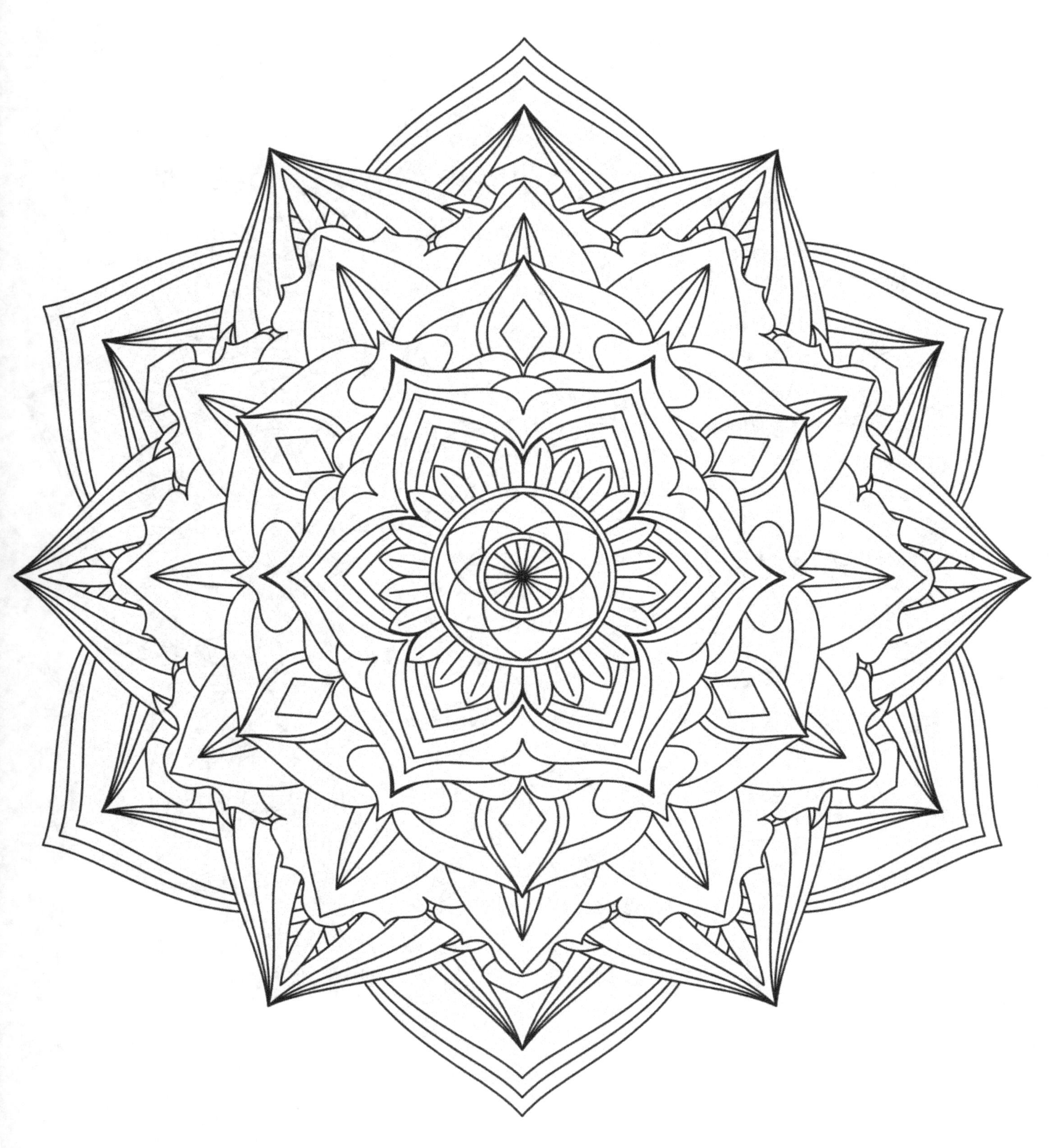

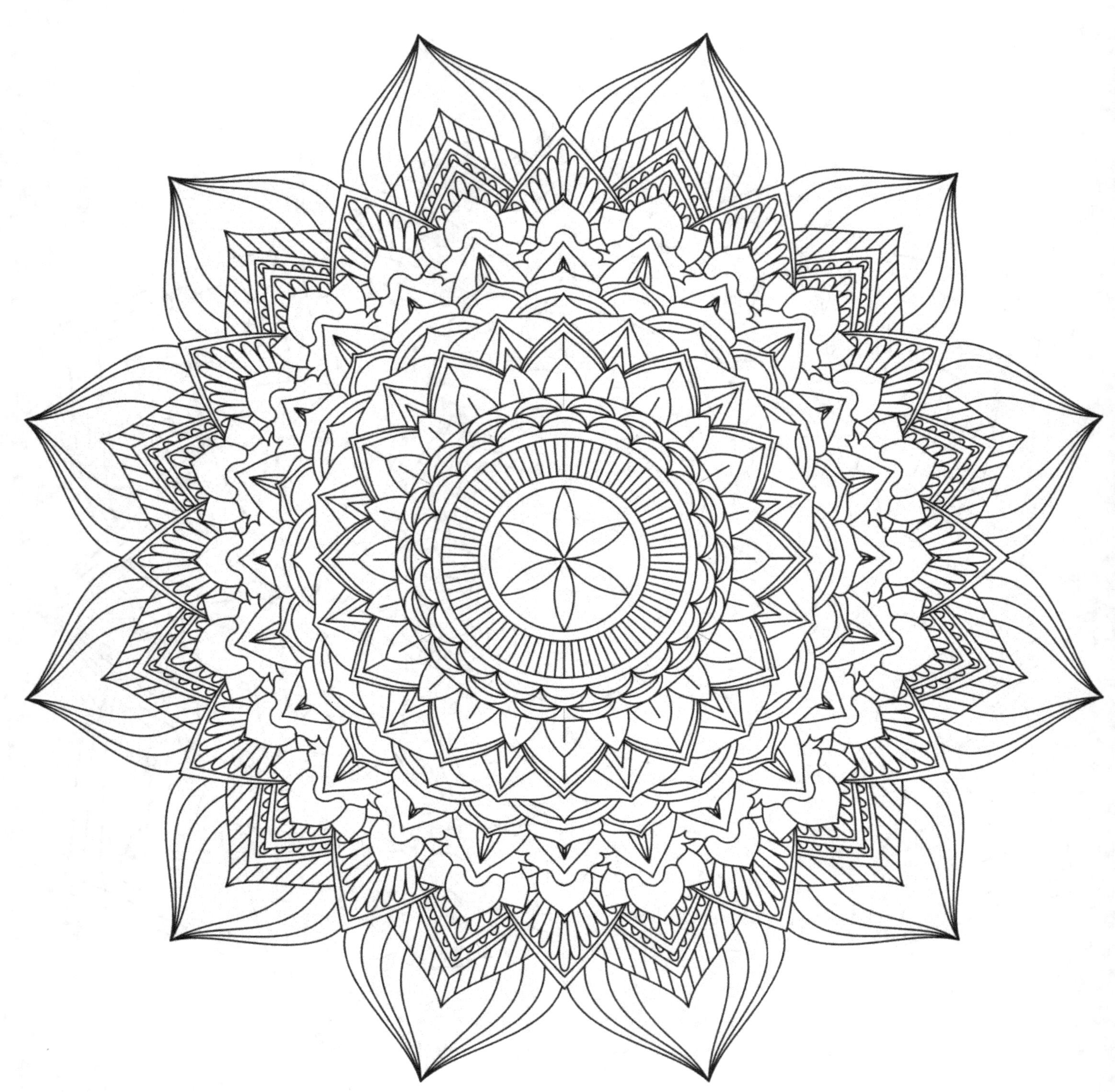

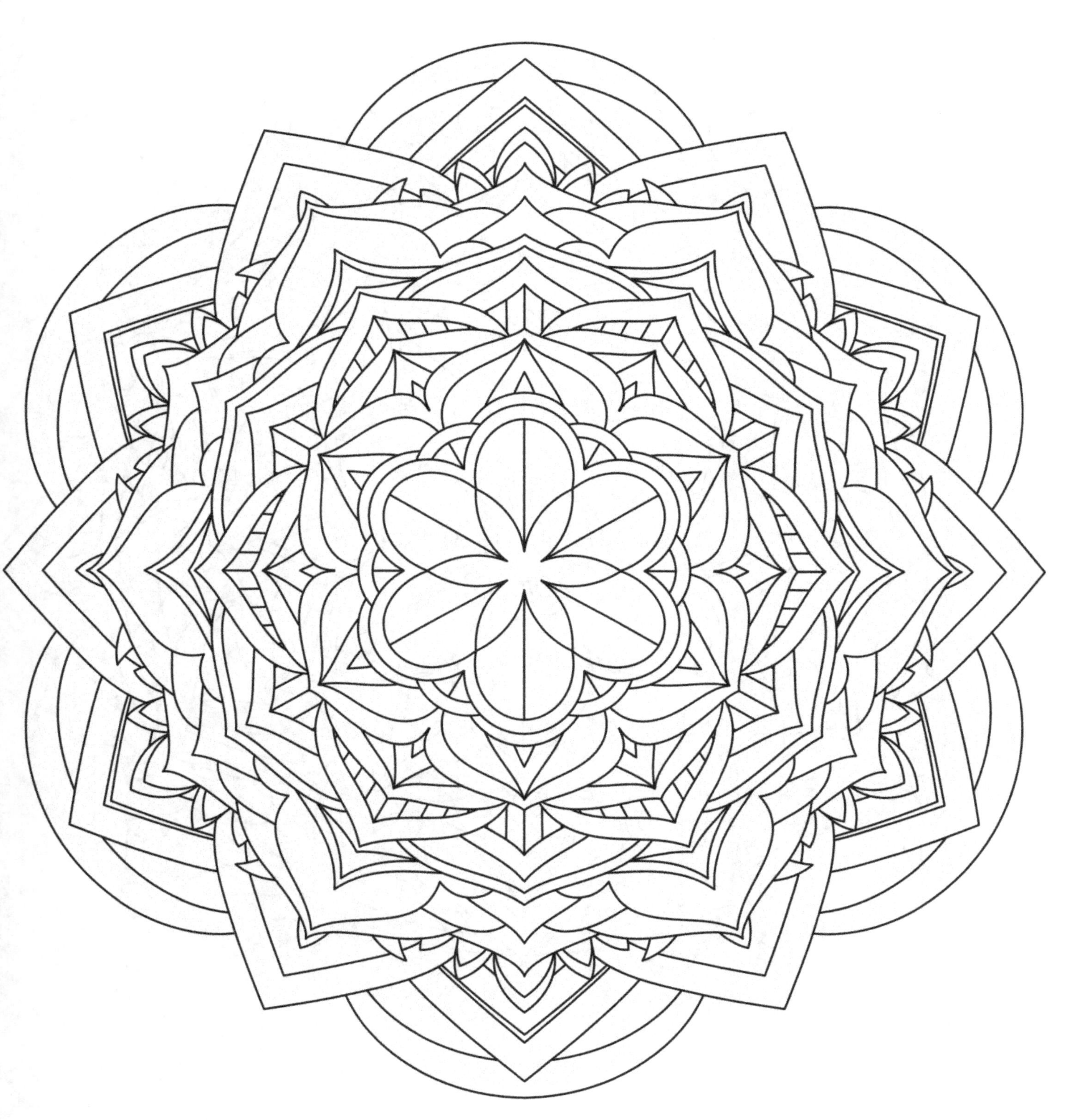

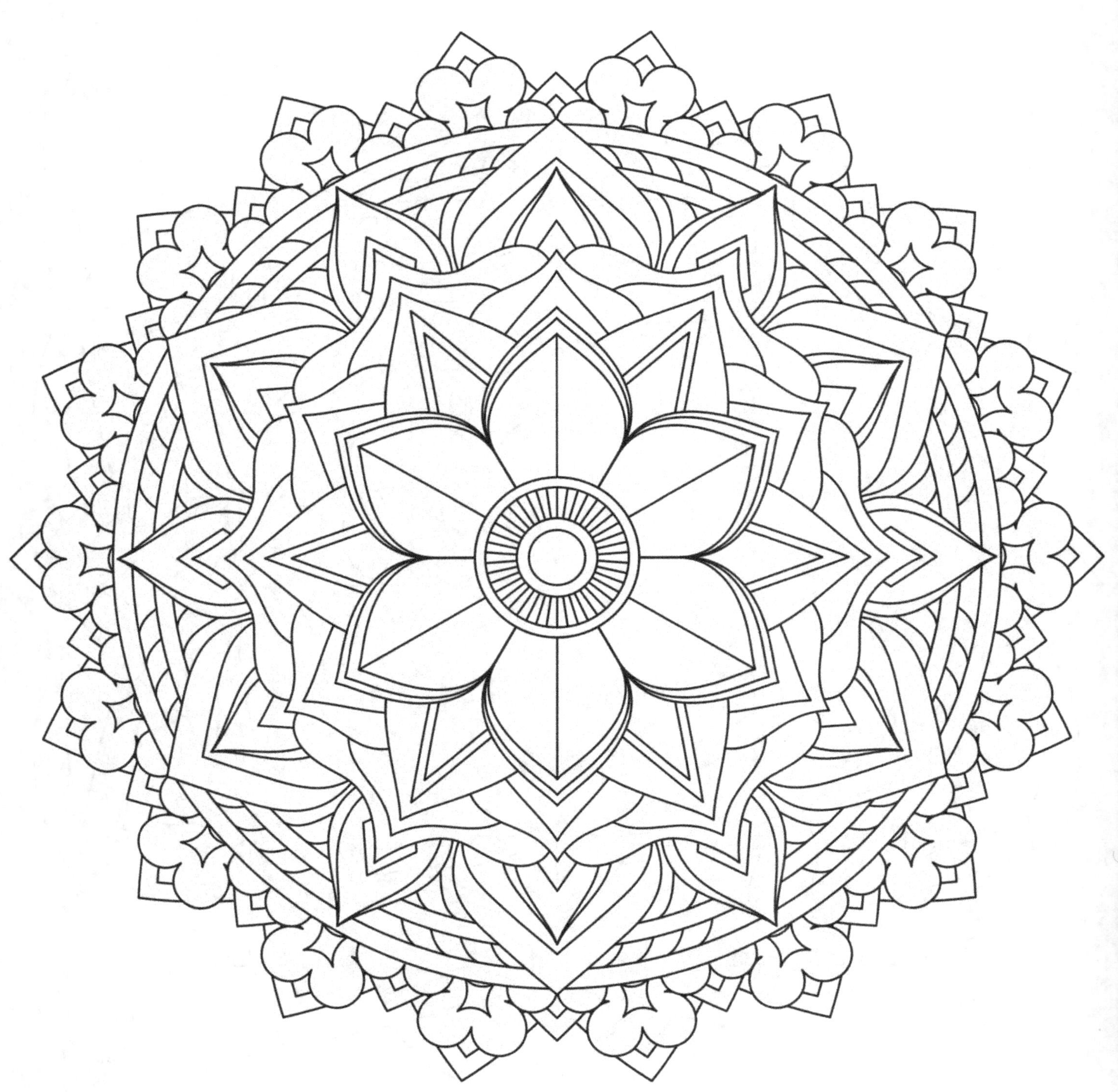

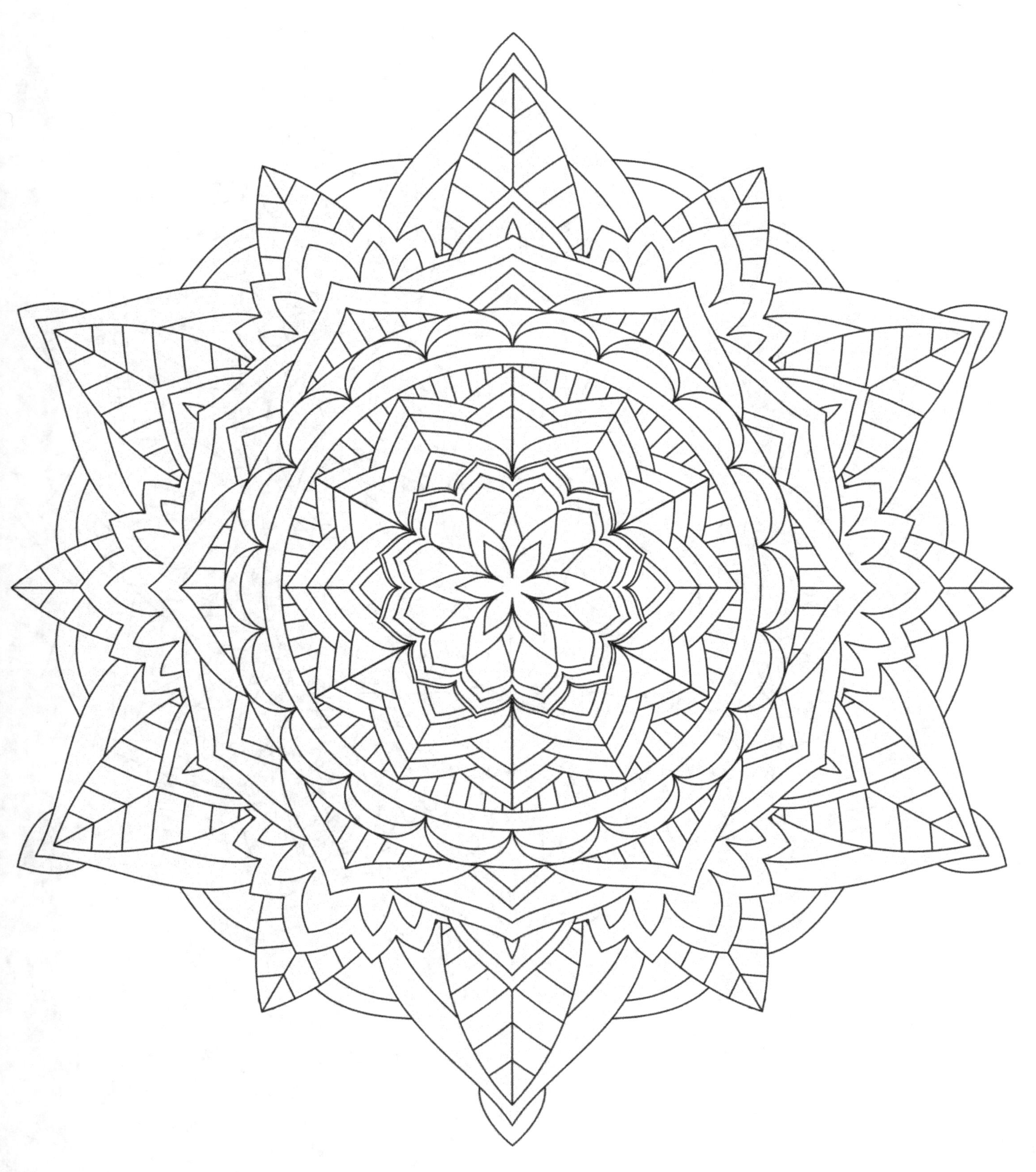

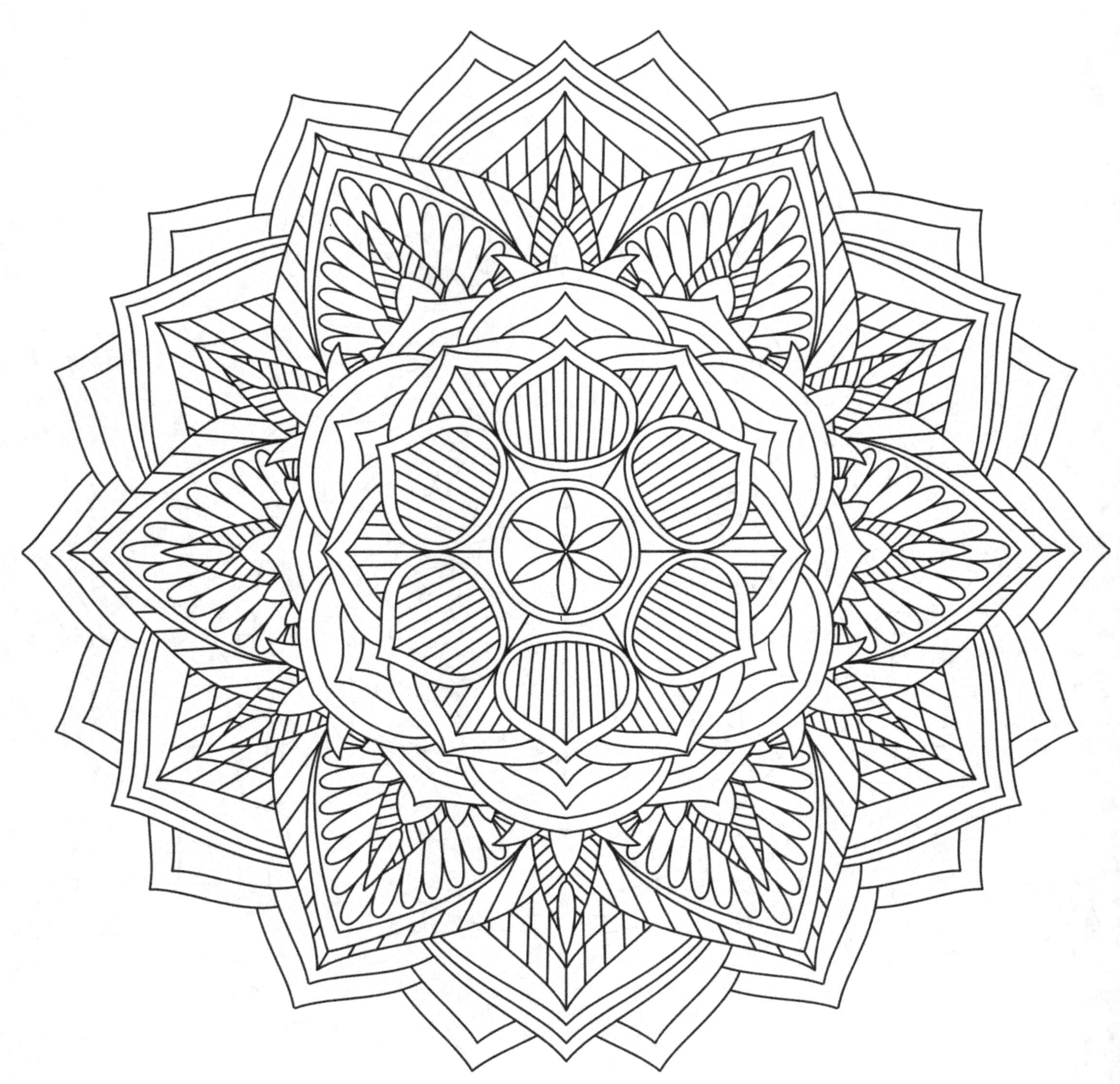

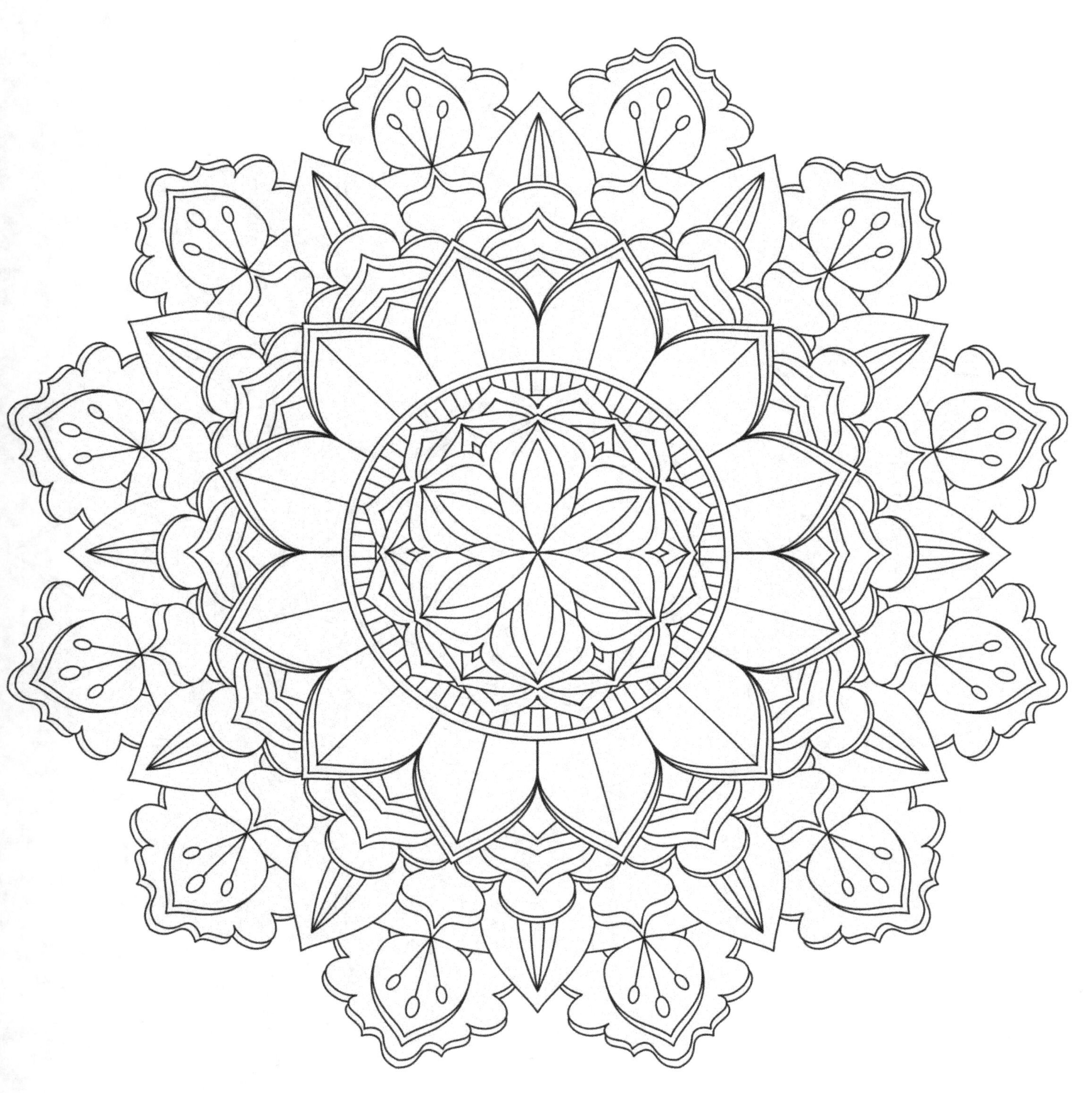

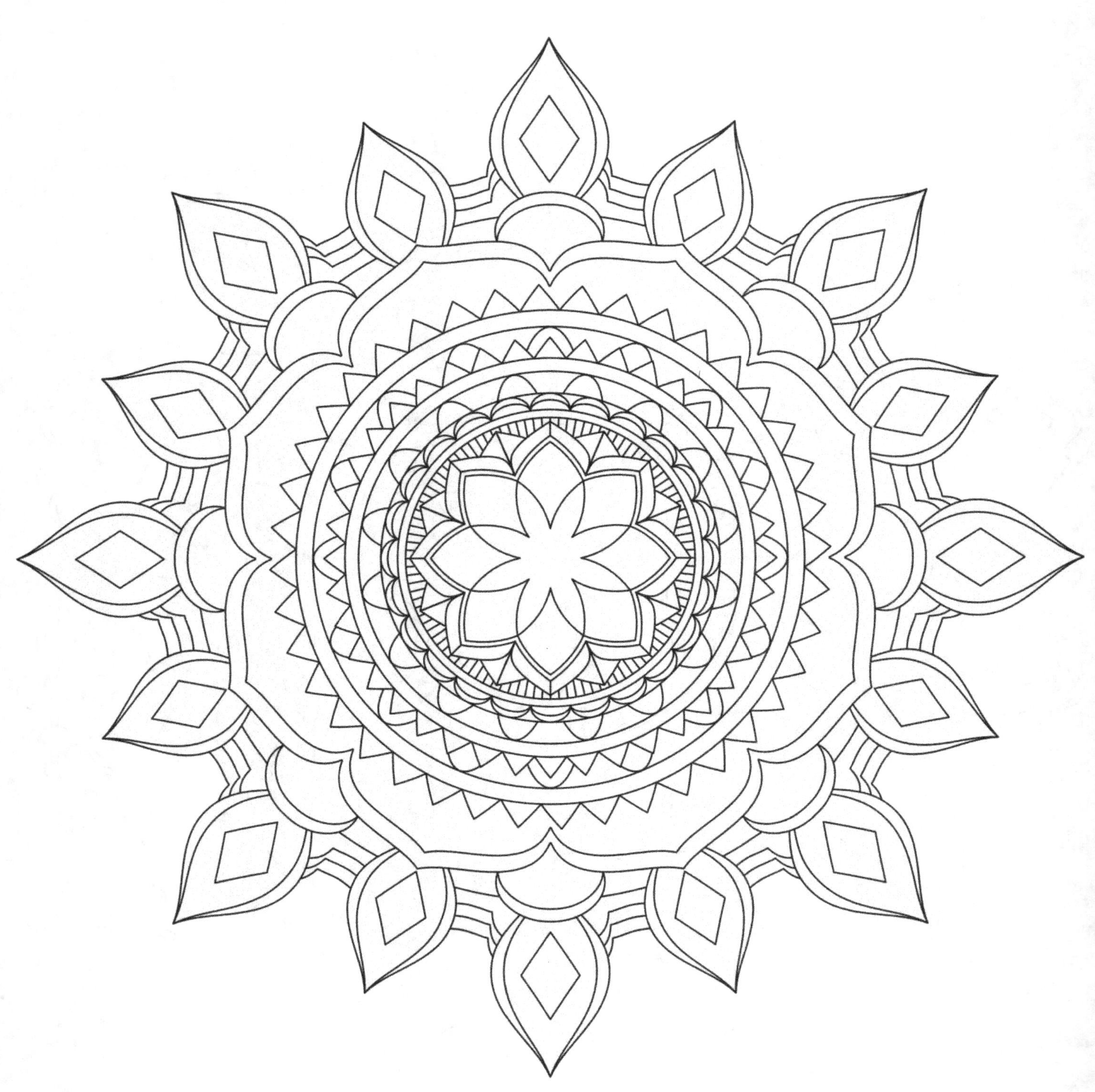

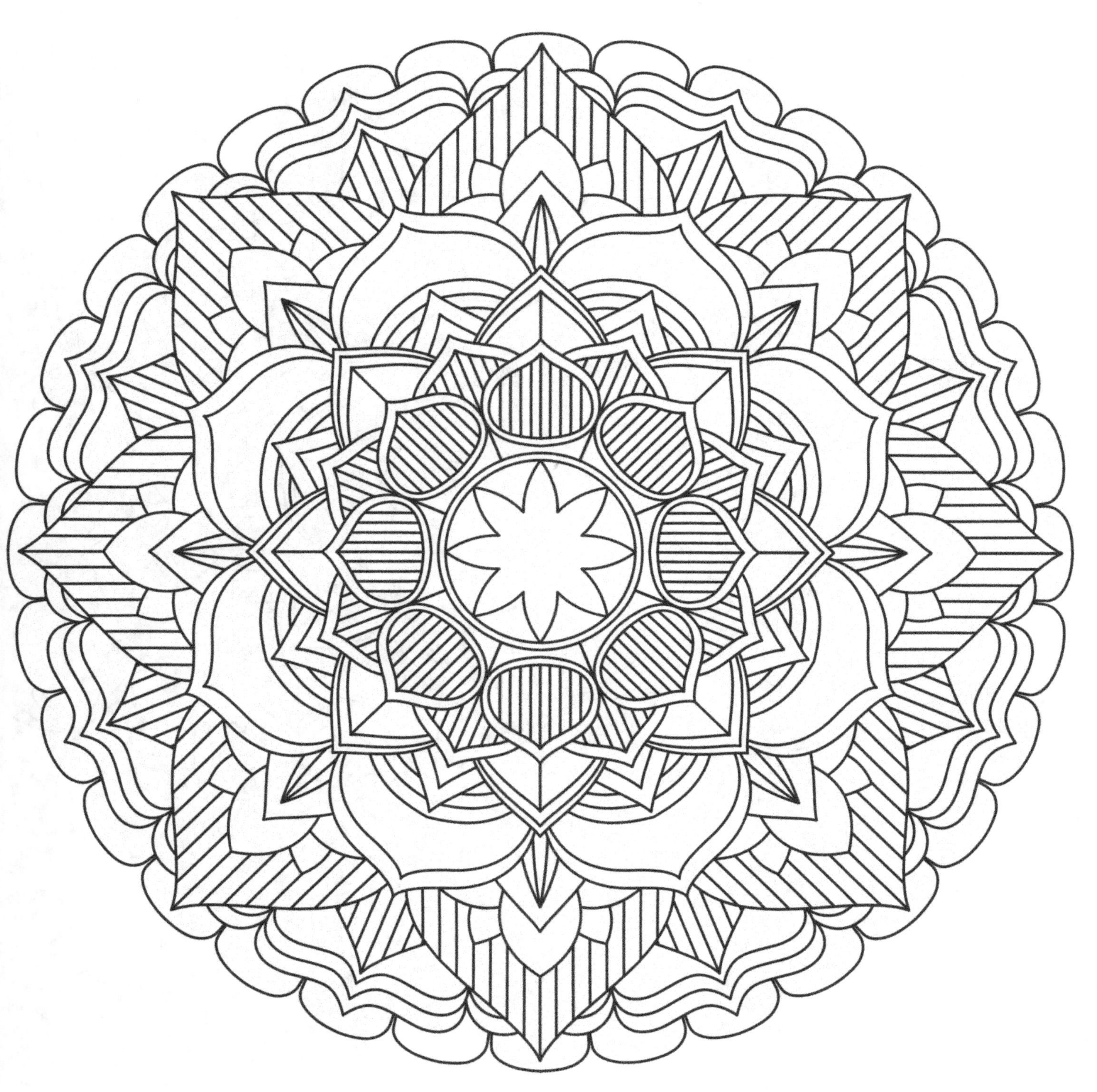

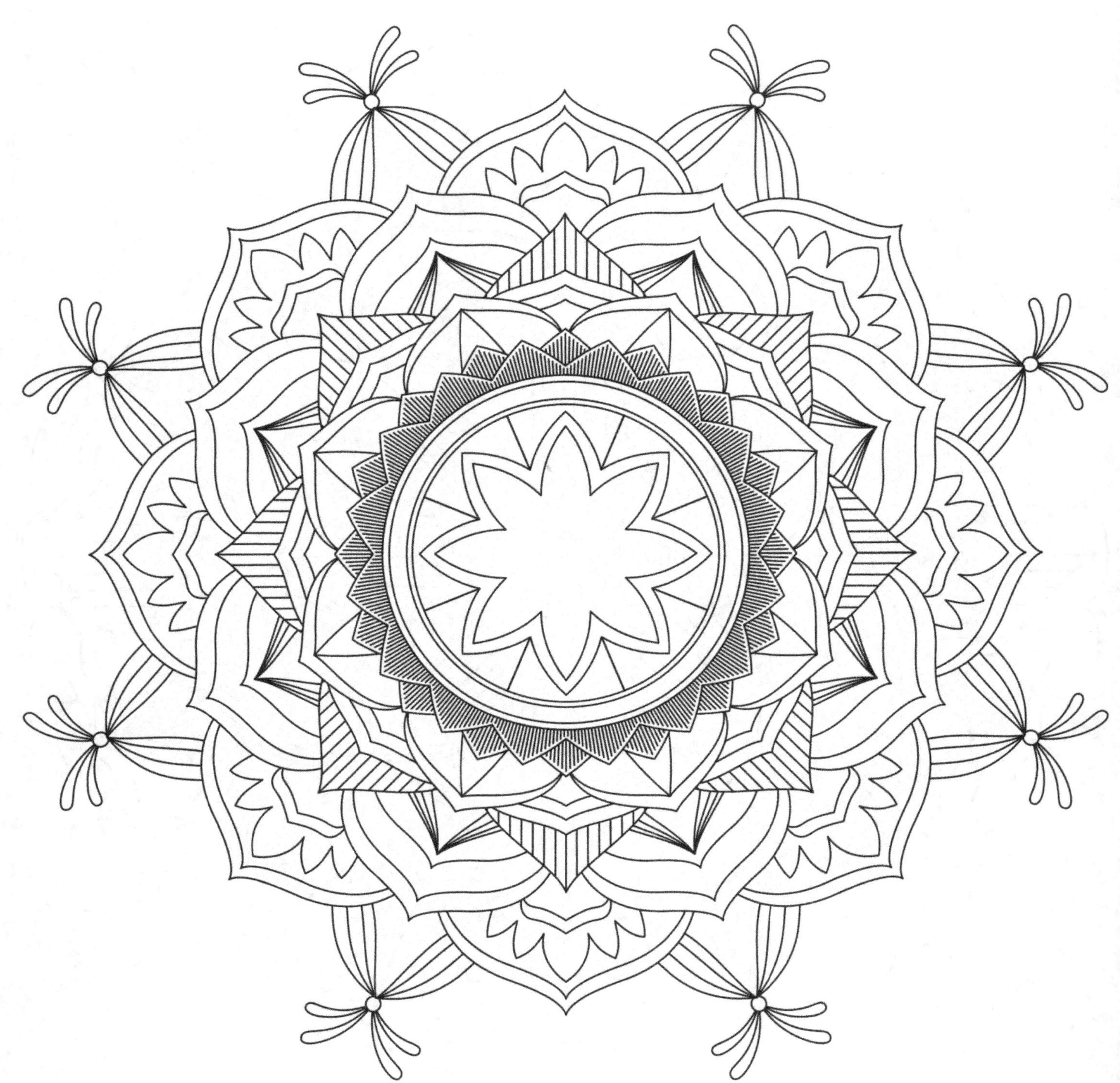

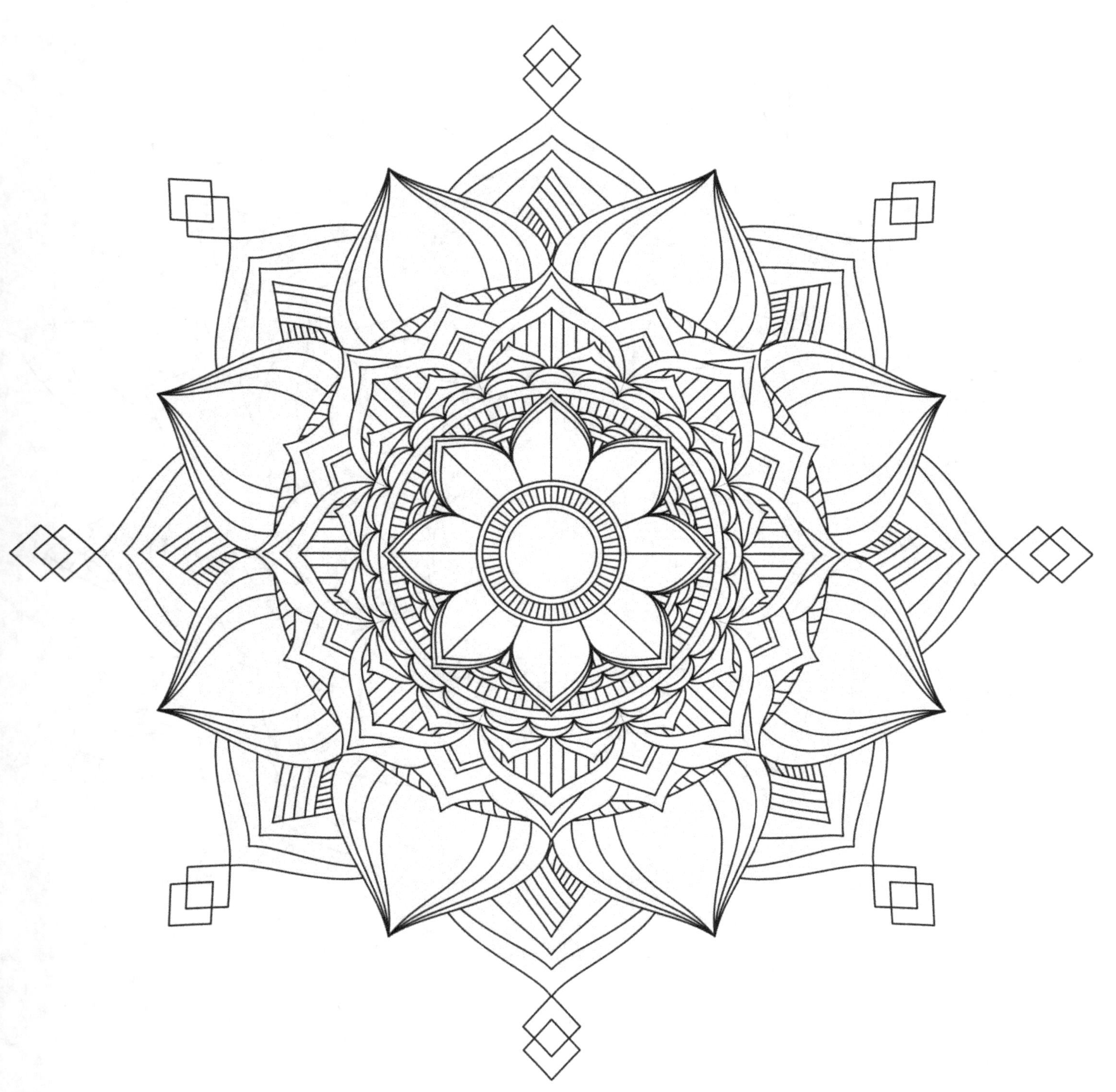

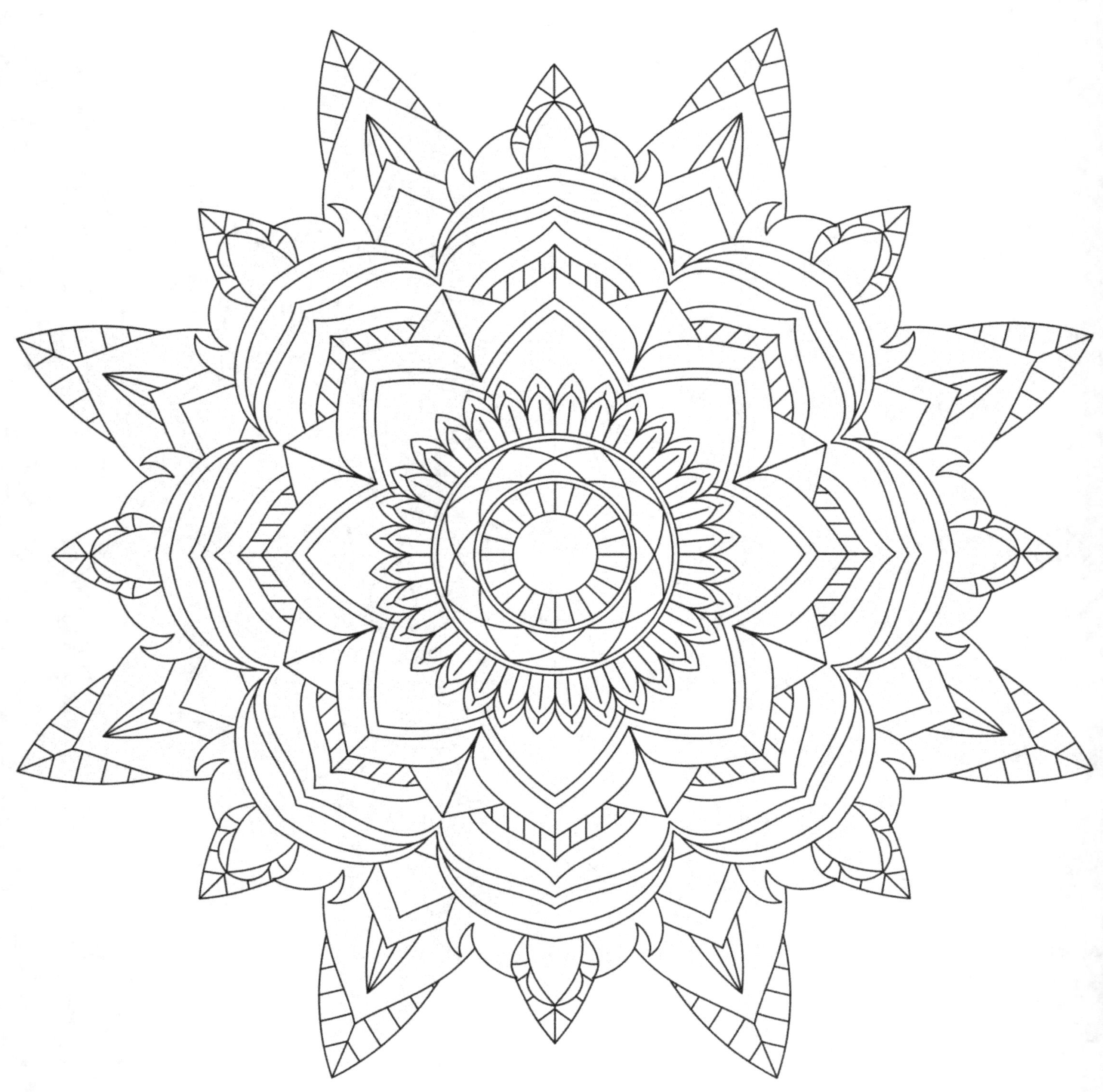

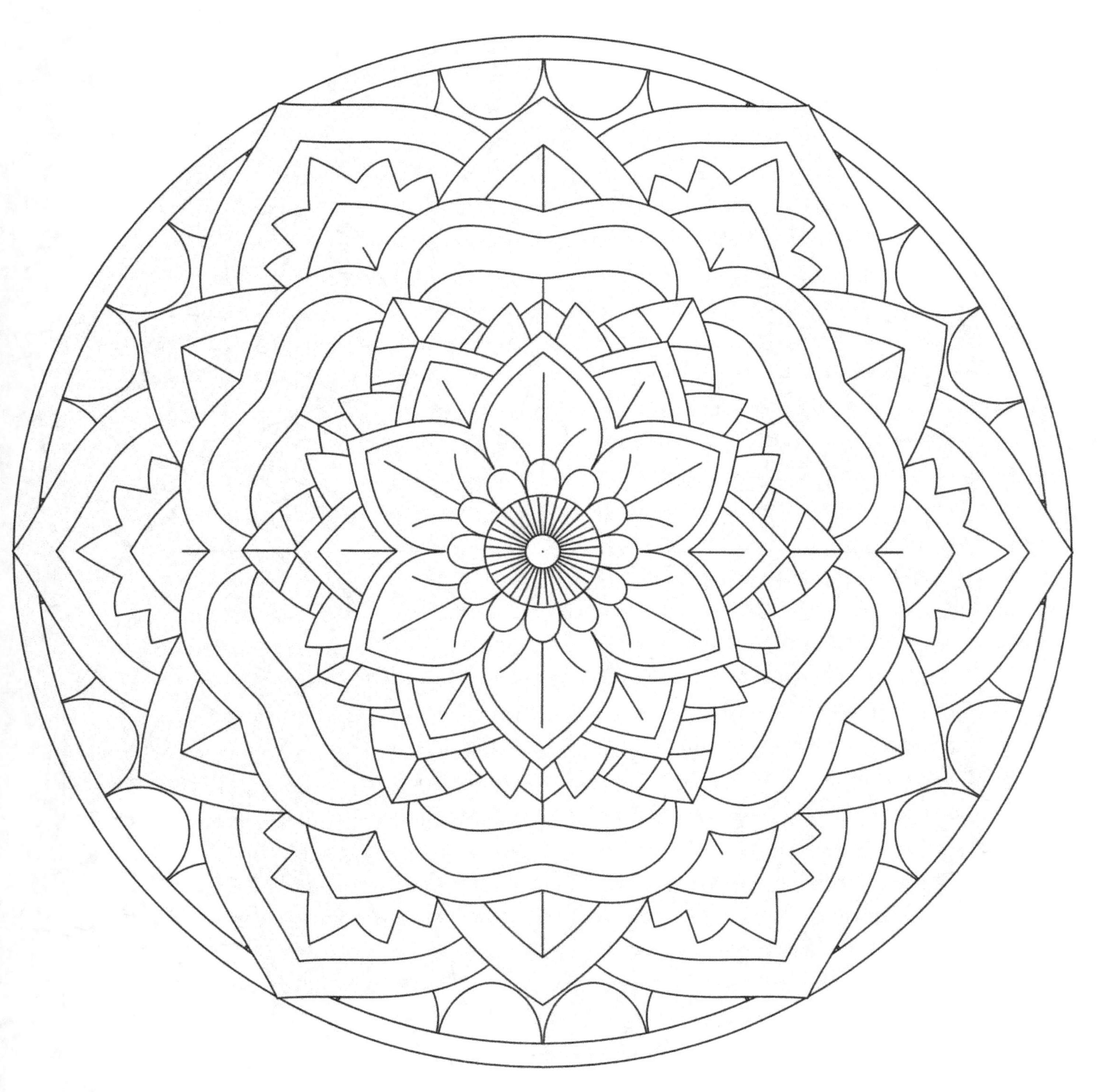

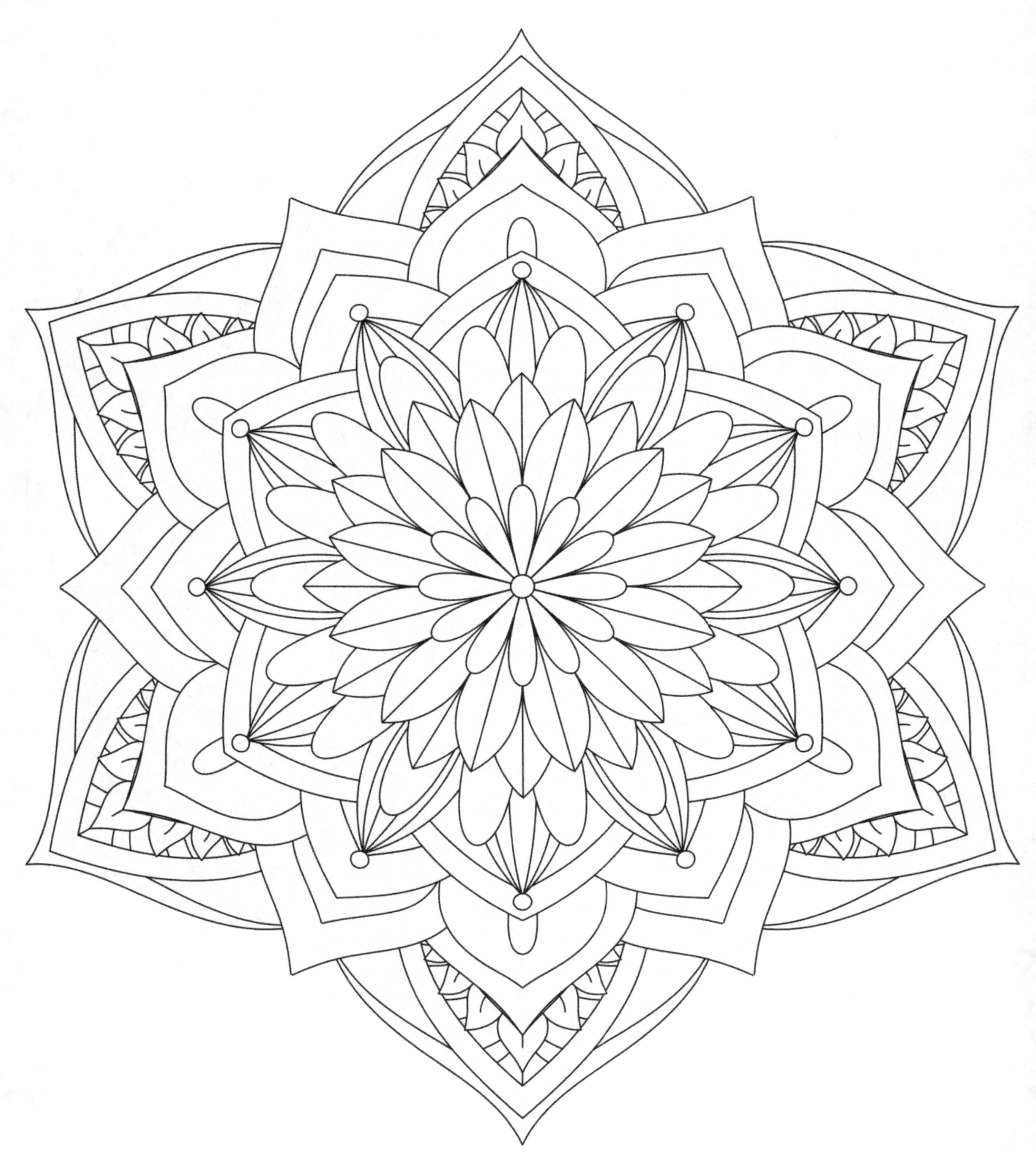

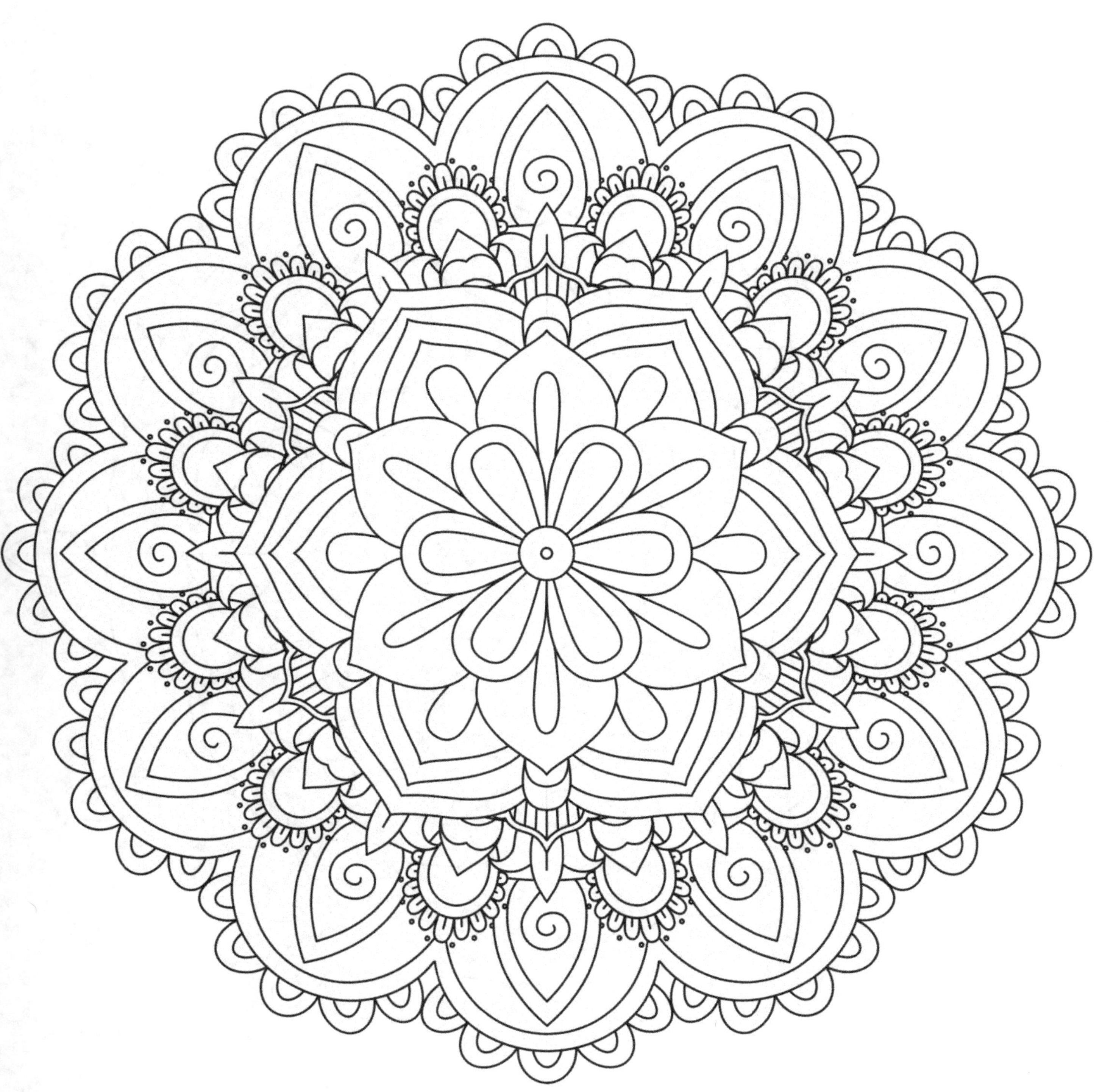

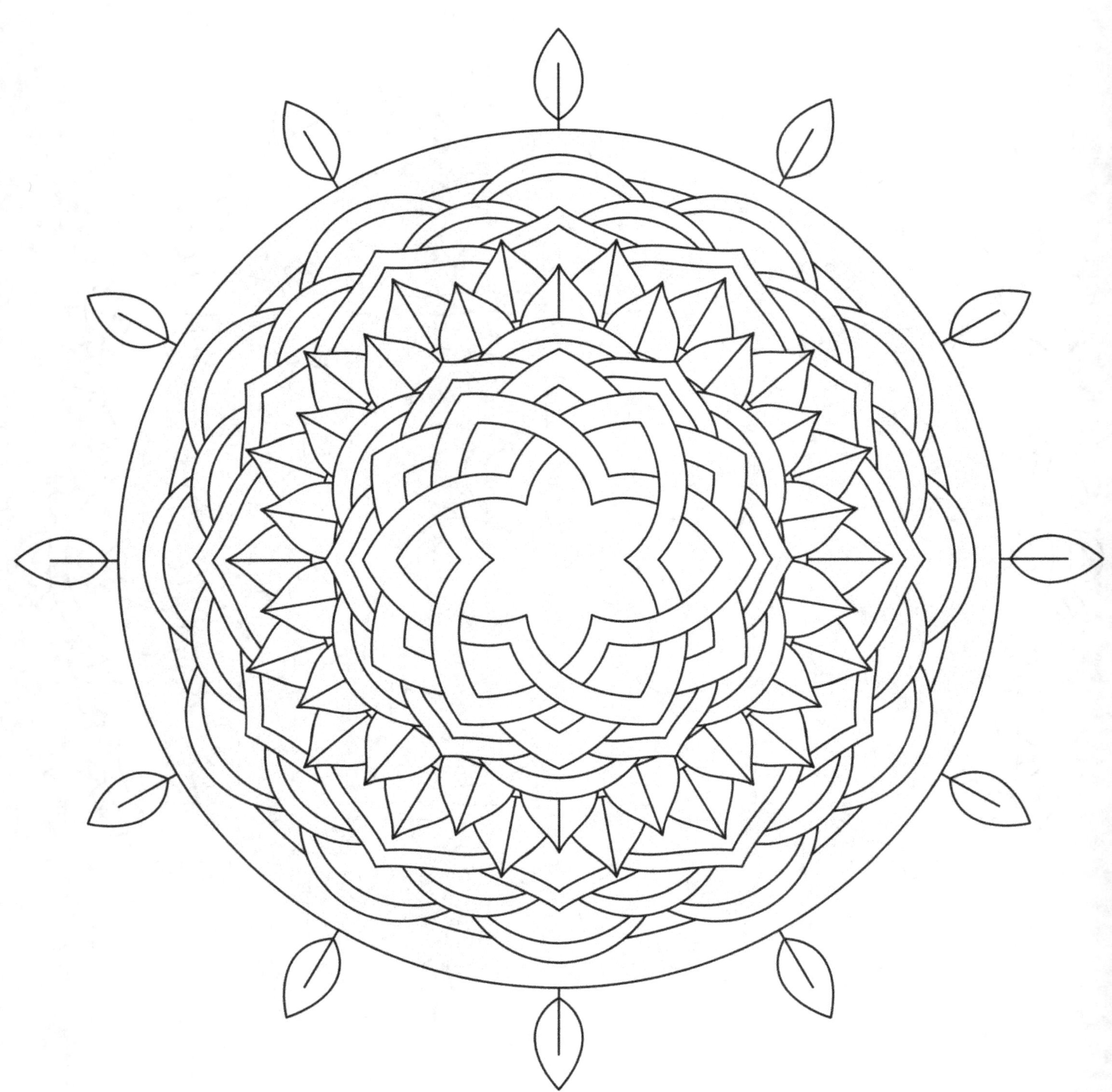

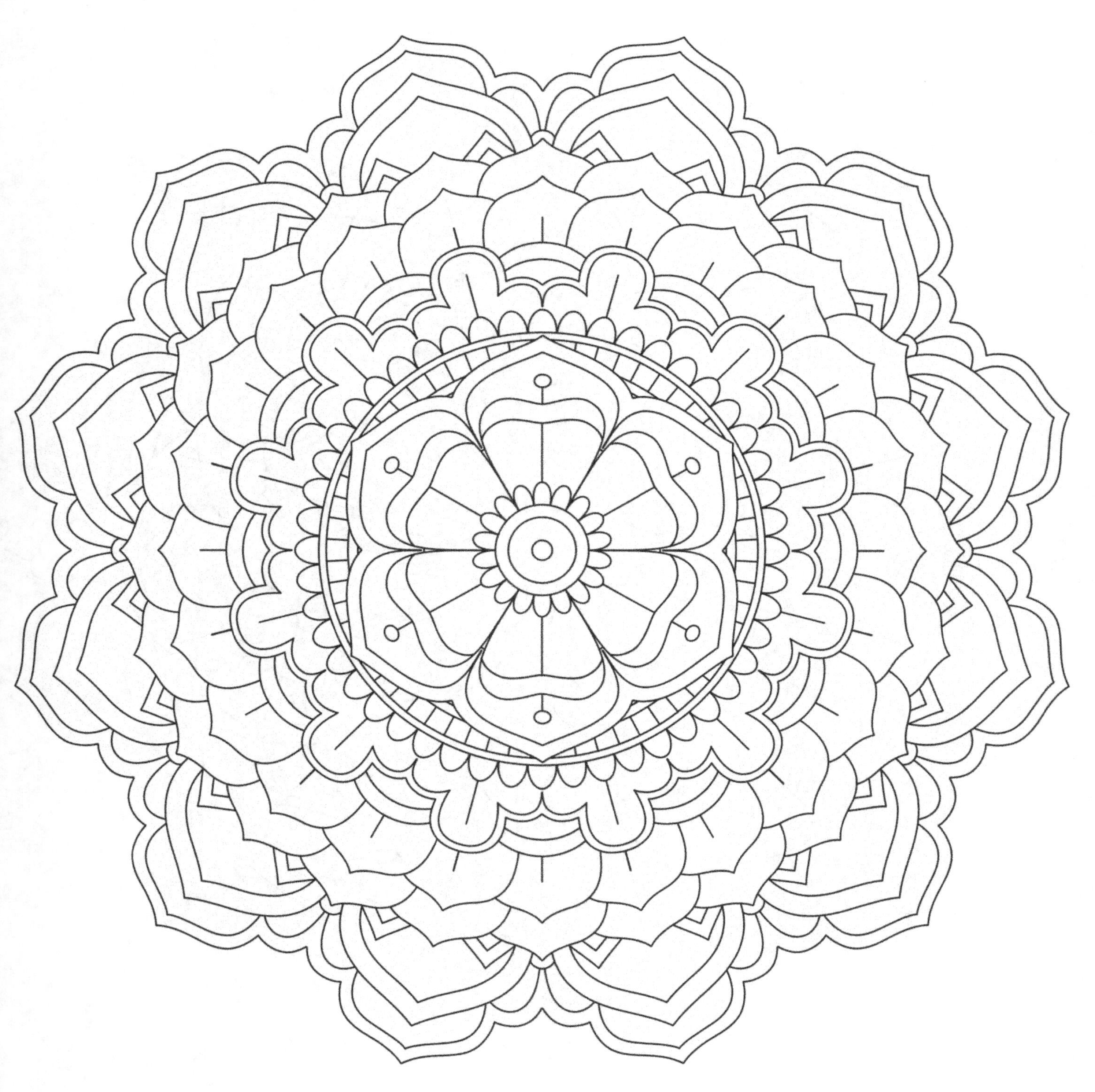

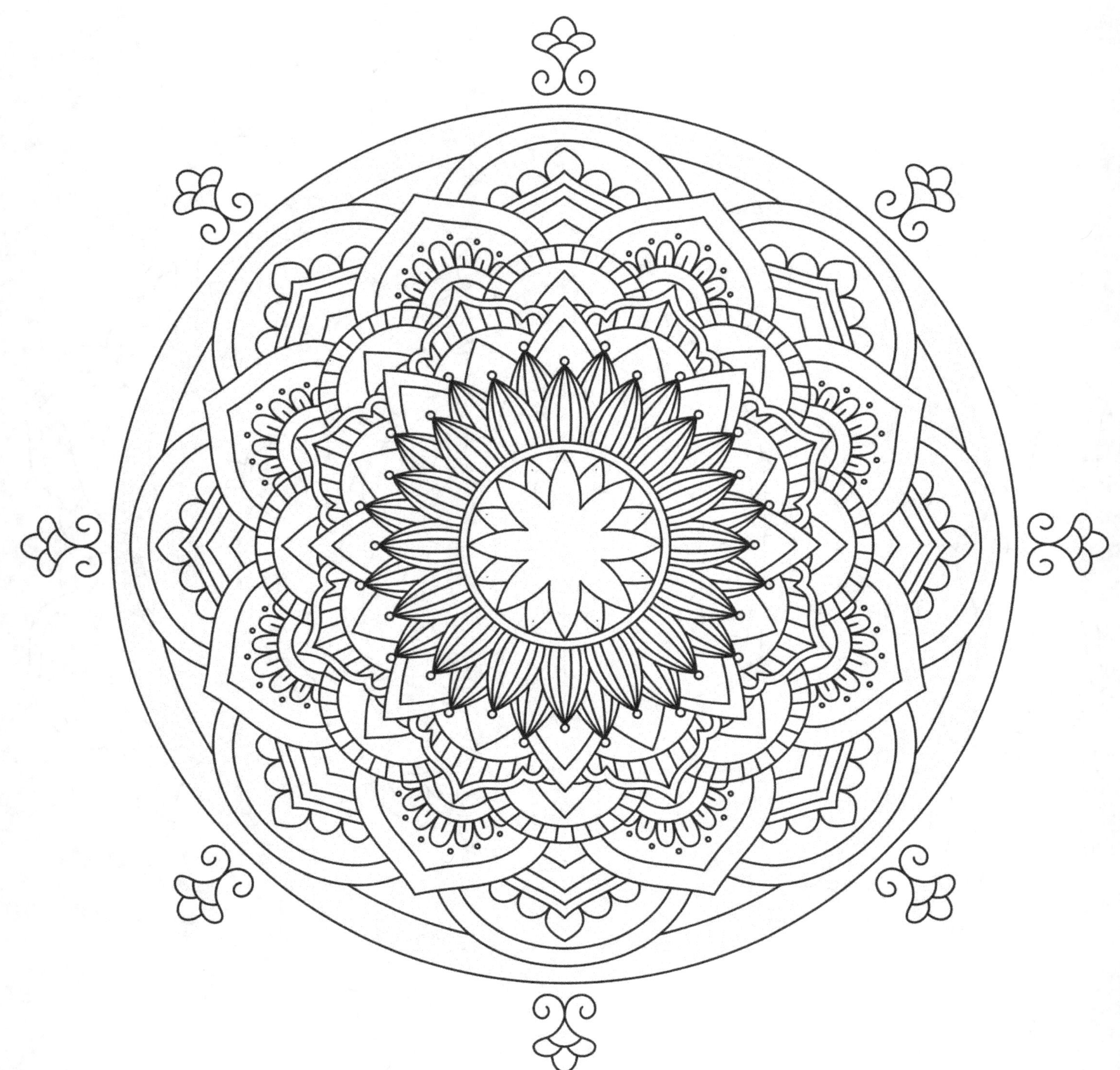

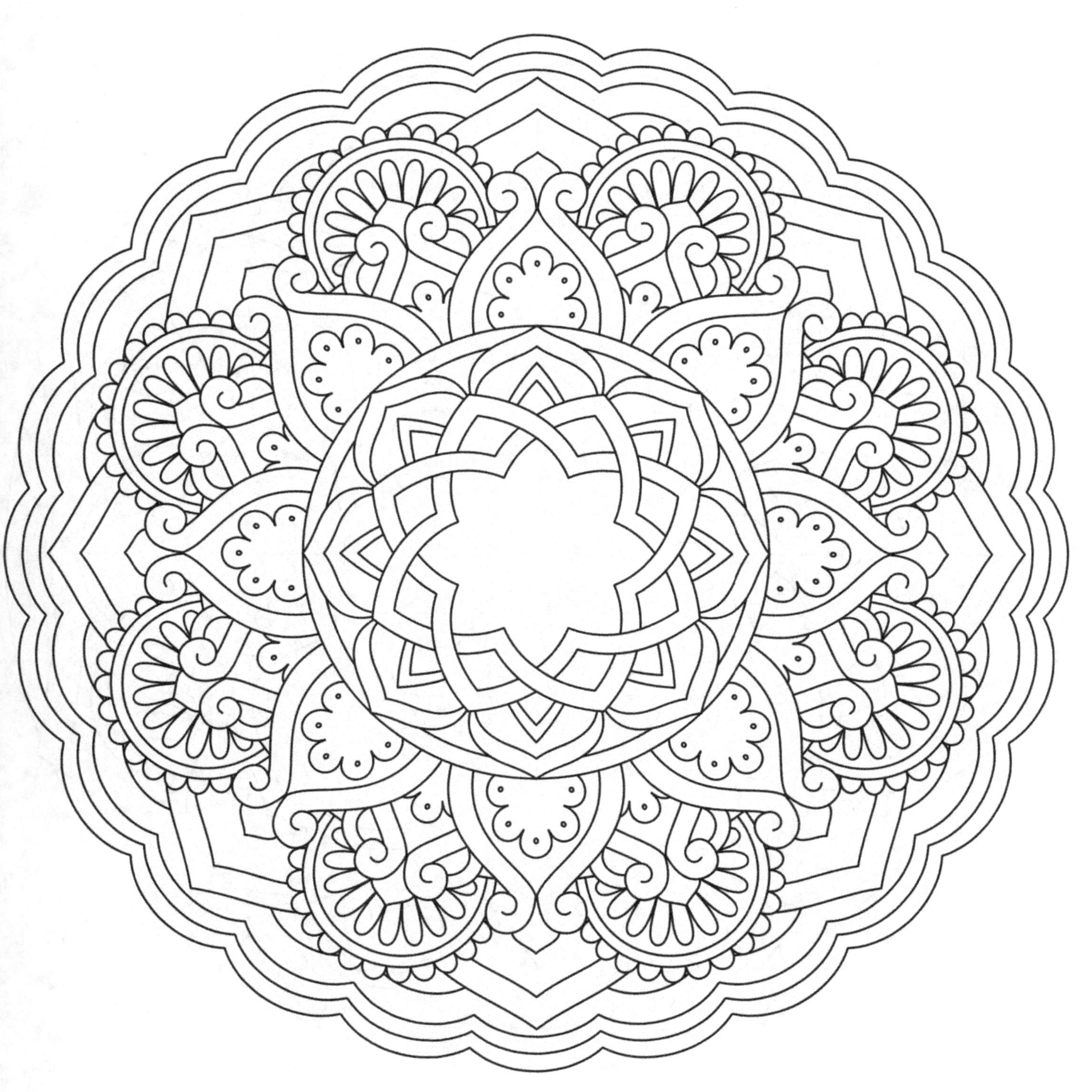

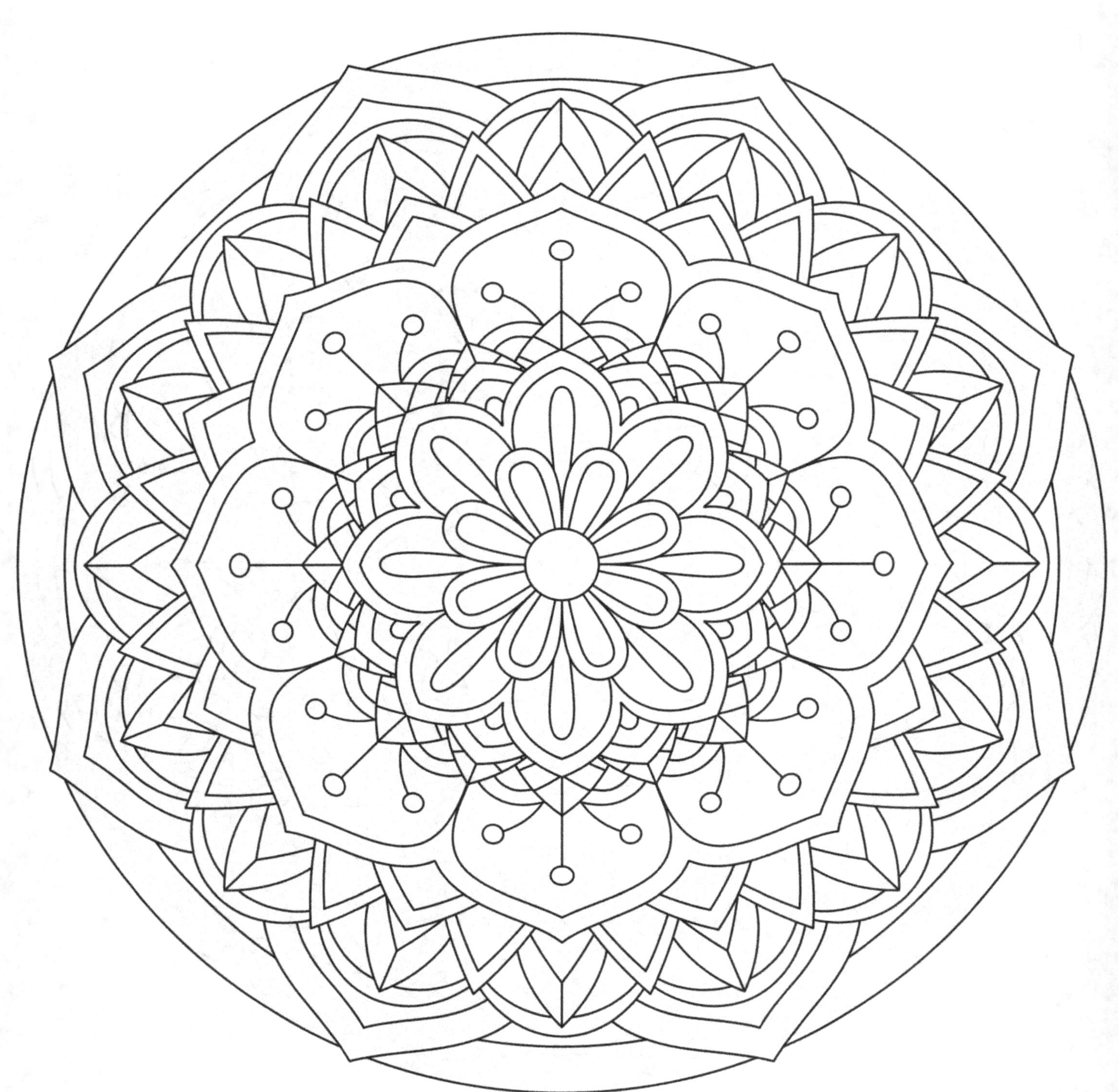

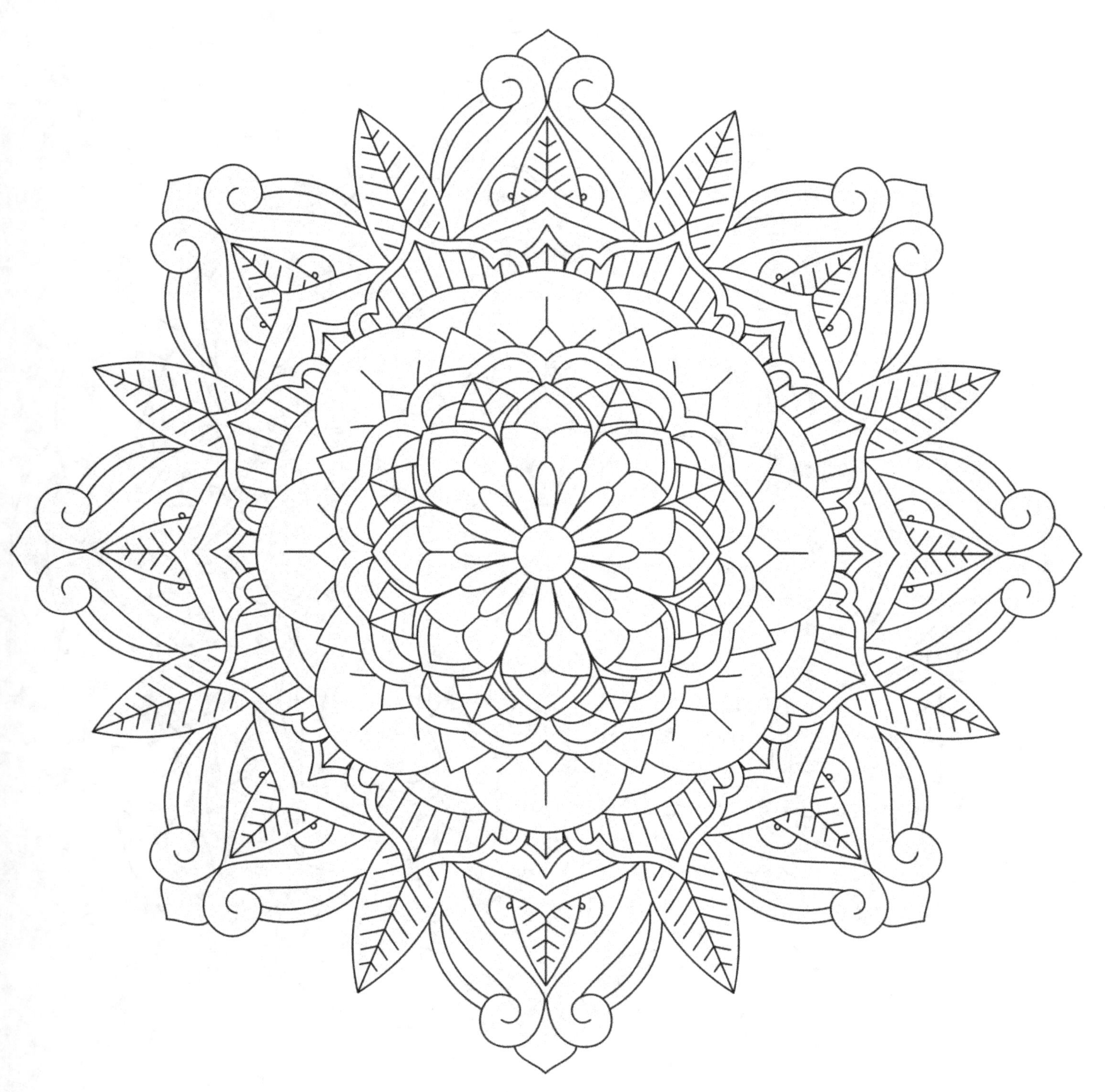

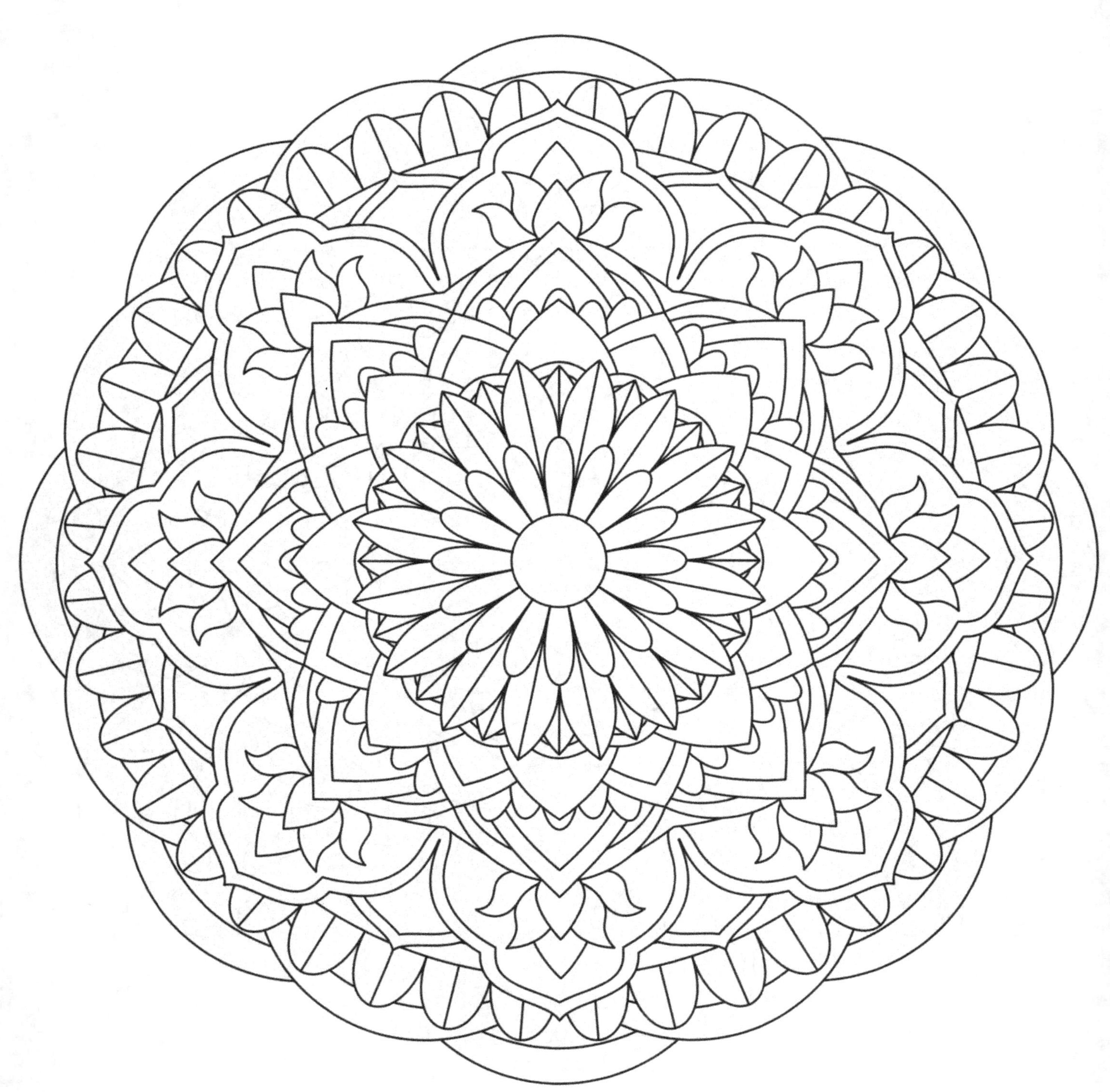

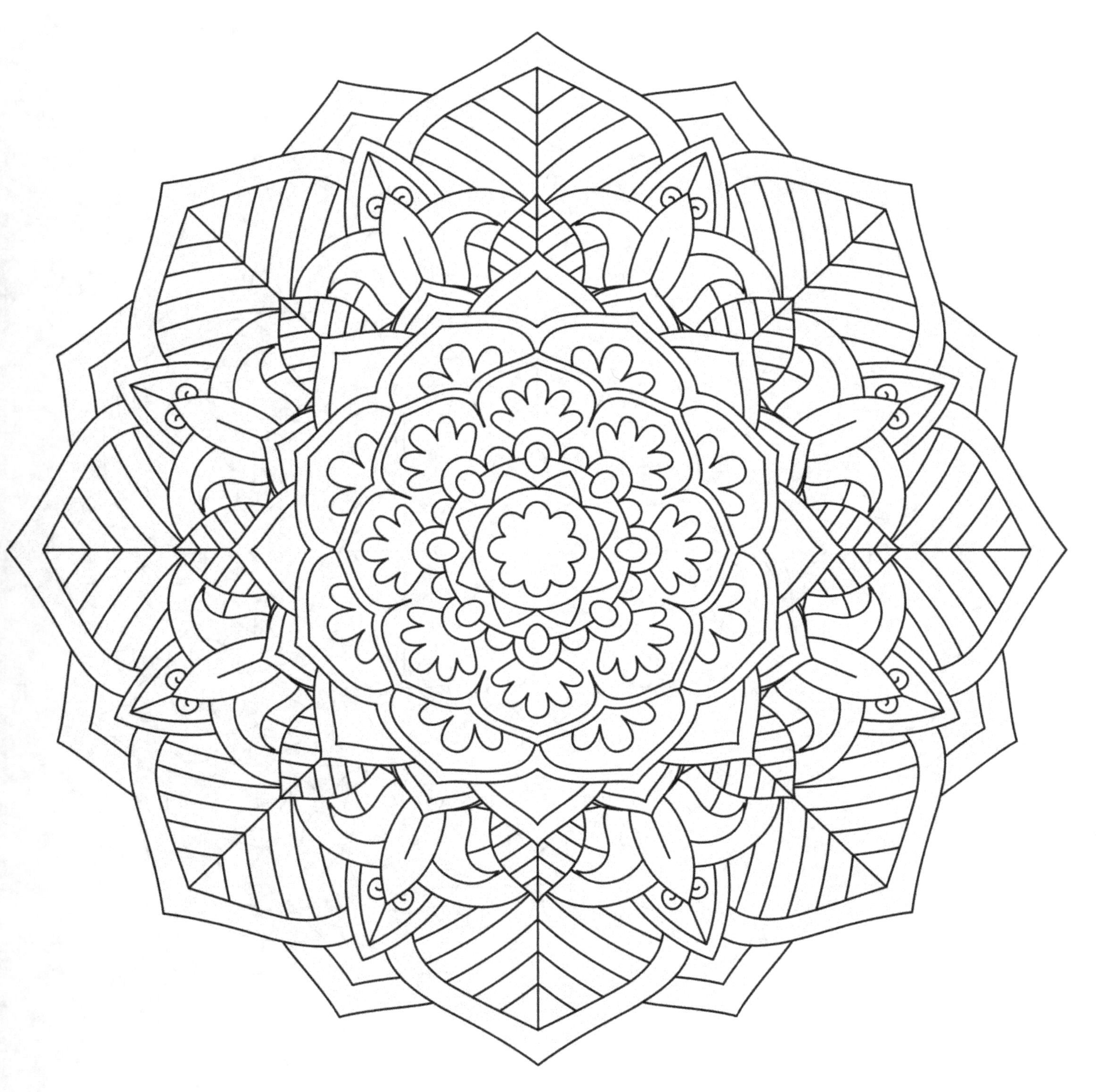

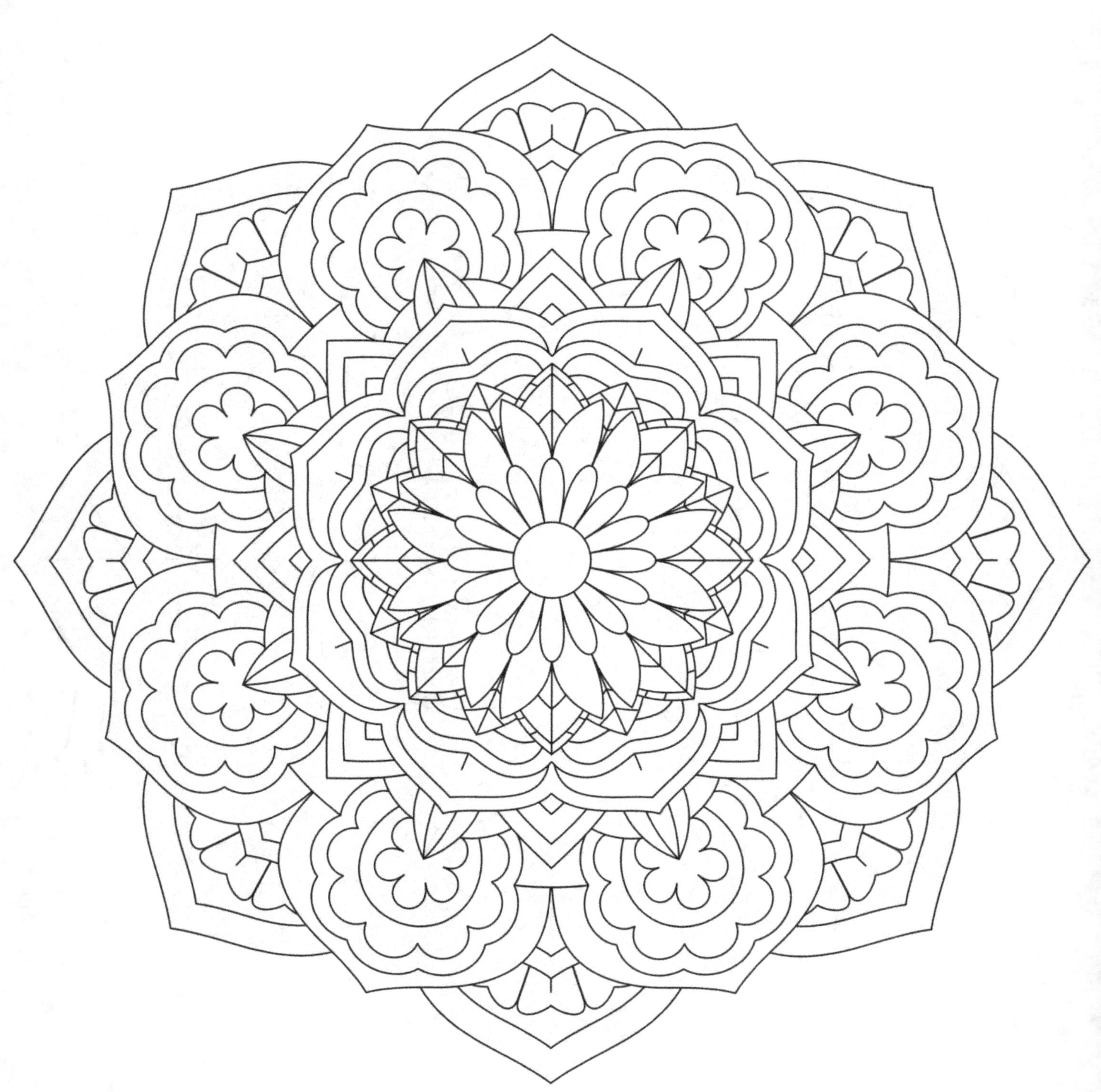

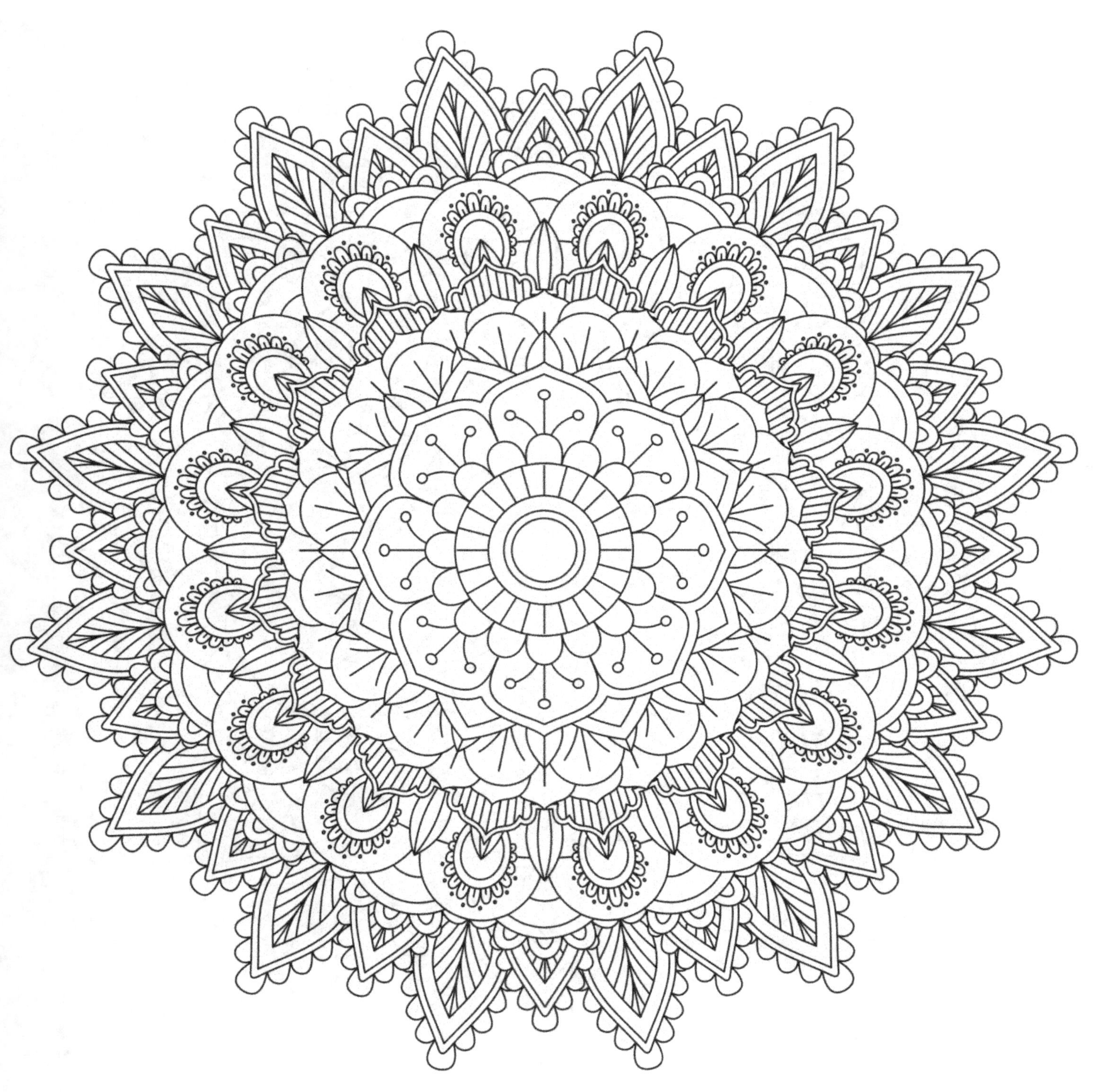

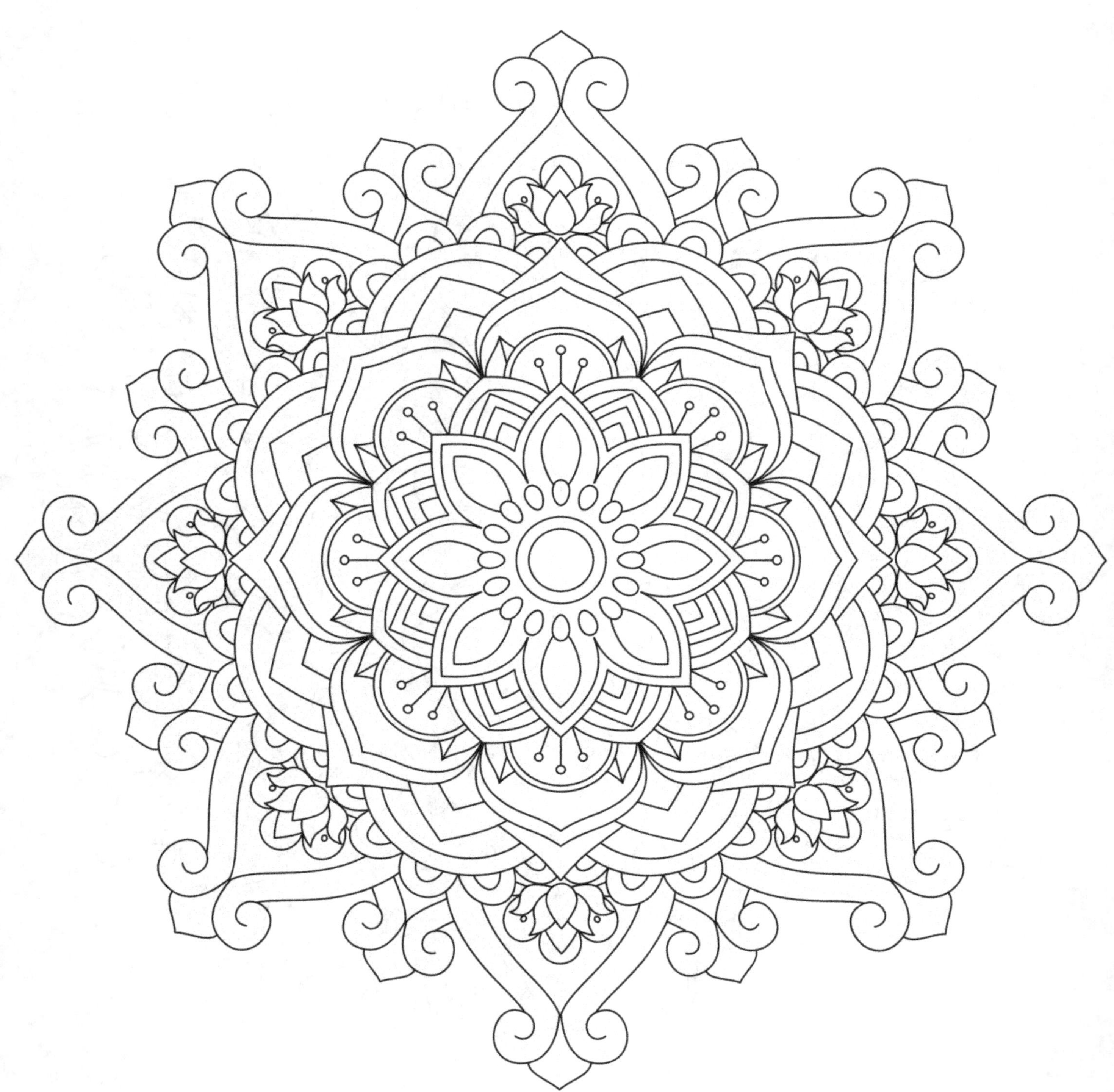

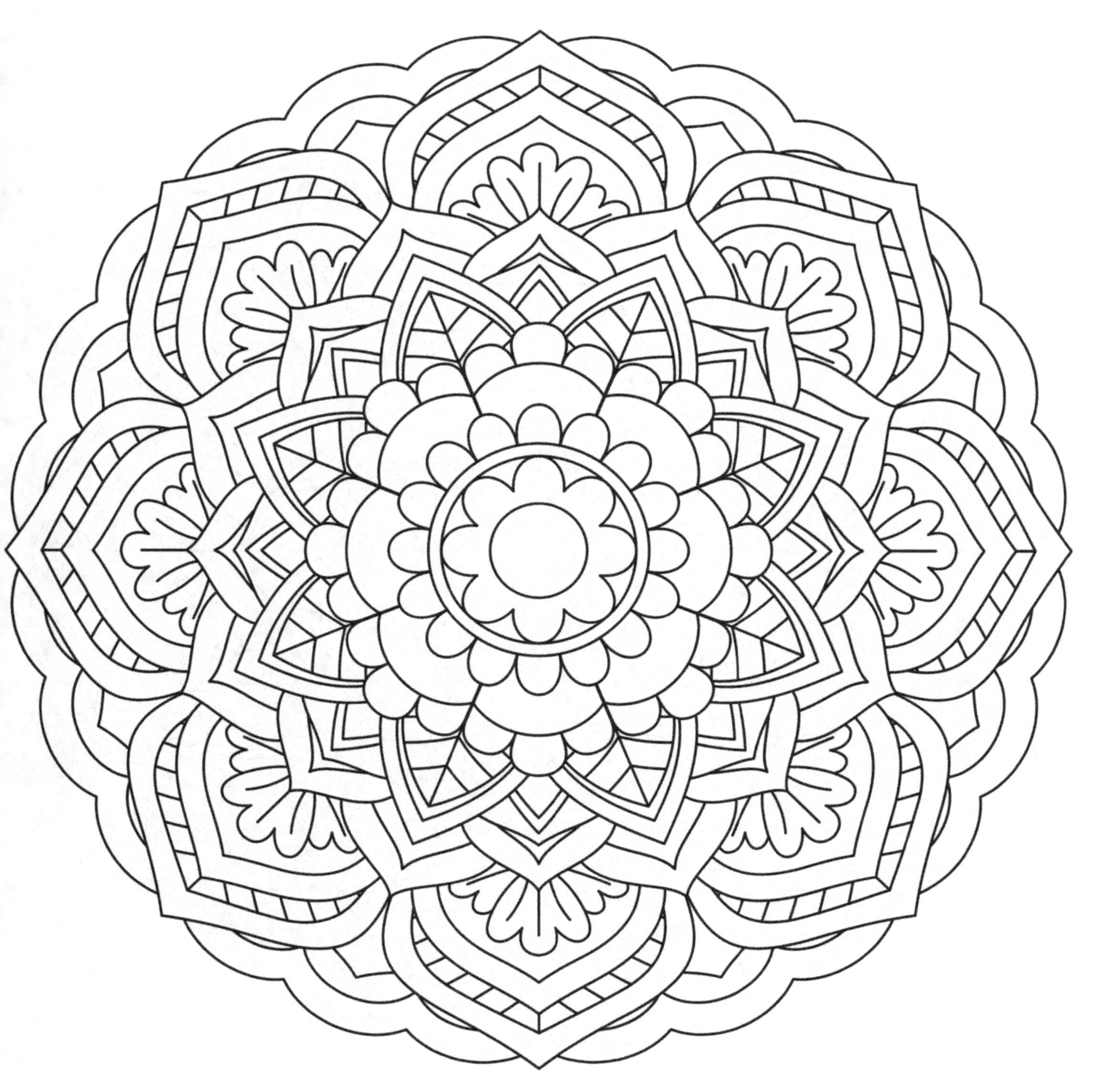

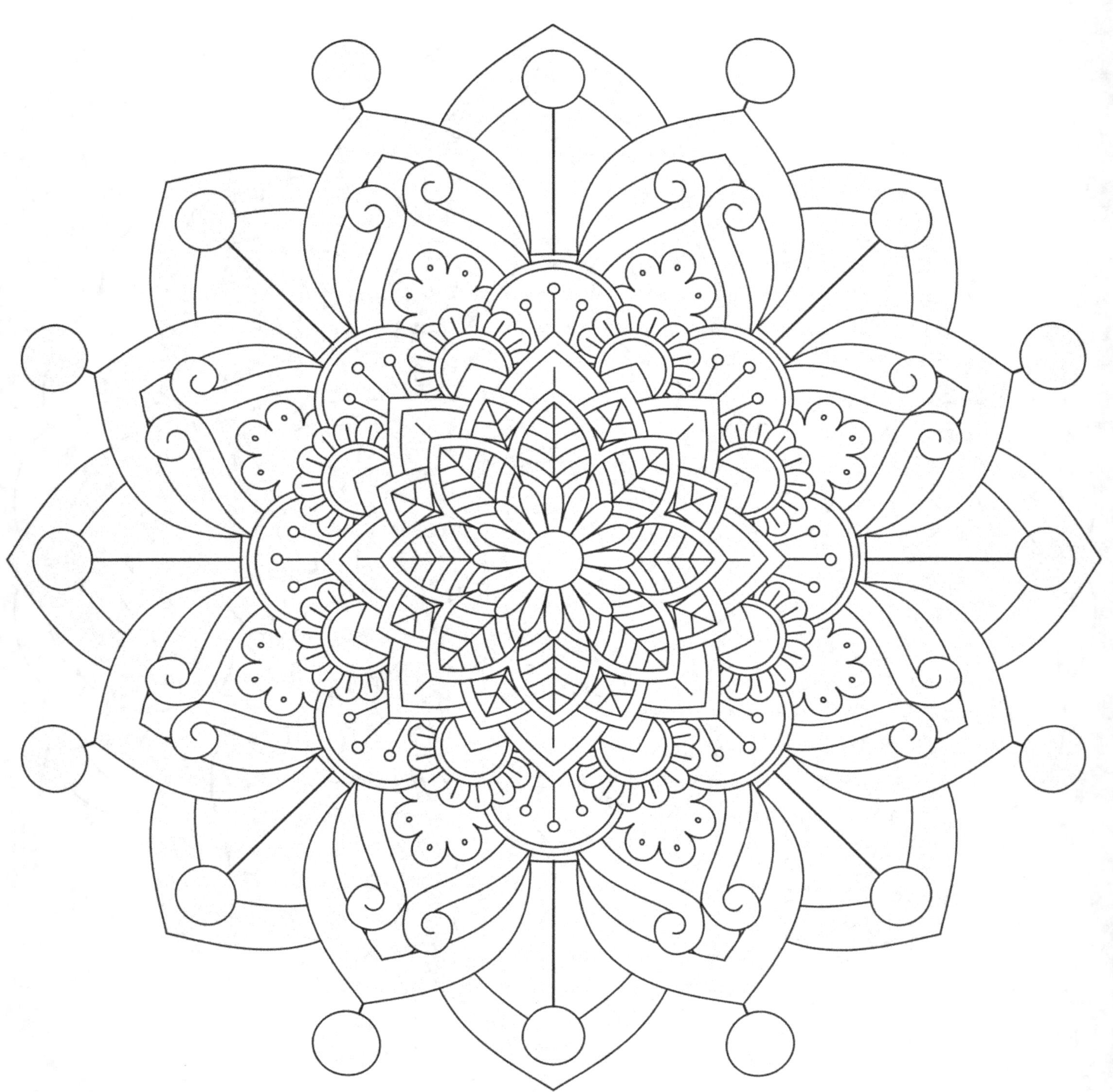

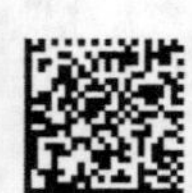

www.ingramcontent.com/pod-product-compliance
Lightning Source LLC
Chambersburg PA
CBHW081603270726
48657CB00029B/3490